15 JOURNEYS WARSAW TO LONDON

Maryla Weinles at the age of 19.

15 JOURNEYS
WARSAW TO LONDON

JASIA REICHARDT

DALKEY ARCHIVE PRESS
CHAMPAIGN • LONDON • DUBLIN

Library of Congress Cataloging-in-Publication Data

Reichardt, Jasia.
15 journeys Warsaw to London / Jasia Reichardt. -- 1st ed.
    p. cm.
ISBN 978-1-56478-720-0 (pbk. : acid-free paper)
1. Reichardt, Jasia--Childhood and youth. 2. Reichardt, Jasia--Travel--Poland.
3. Reichardt, Jasia--Family. 4. Chaykin, Maryla--Correspondence. 5. Themerson,
Franciszka--Correspondence. 6. World War, 1939-1945--Personal narratives,
Jewish. 7. World War, 1939-1945--Jews--Poland--Warsaw. 8. Jewish children in
the Holocaust--Poland--Warsaw. 9. Jews--Poland--Warsaw--Biography. 10. Jews,
Polish--Biography. I. Title. II. Title: Fifteen journeys.
DS134.72.R44A3 2012
940.53'18092--dc23
                              2012004097

Partially funded by a grant from the Illinois Arts Council, a state agency

www.dalkeyarchive.com

Cover: design and composition by Nick Wadley
Printed on permanent/durable acid-free paper and bound in the United States of
America

CONTENTS

The Weinles family: Jakub, Maryla, Łucja, Warsaw, 1906

Jakub, Maryla, Franciszka, Łucja, Warsaw, c. 1909

INTRODUCTION

This is a wartime story of a family conjured from letters and memories. It is my story inasmuch as I am here to tell it, but since it deals principally with the years 1939–1946, and I was born in 1933, it is the story of a child. It takes place during the Second World War in Poland, mainly in Warsaw.

The letters are those of my family; the memories are mine. In the letters, there are many repetitions, because nobody could tell if all or any of them would reach their destinations. They are often written in code or metaphor, some are marked in pencil by the censor, and there are some with lines excised.

Most of the letters quoted here were written by my mother, Maryla Chaykin, and my grandmother, Łucja Weinles, to Franciszka Themerson, their sister and daughter, respectively. At the very beginning of the correspondence, Franciszka is in Paris, and then in London from 1940 on.

In 1988, a few days before she died, Franciszka Themerson was lying on a bed in her studio in Warrington Crescent in

London's Maida Vale. She turned to me and pointed to a grey box file on a shelf. 'Your mother's letters', she said.

Of course I knew they were there, but I didn't want to see them.

I waited. And so did the unopened box, now on a different shelf. Years passed, and eventually the right moment came for me to open the box, not without trepidation, and—how shall I put it—to face the music, and if not exactly to dance, at least to tell this story.

The story unfolds slowly. The letters from the grey box are translated and appear here in the order they were written, with my own interventions between. It is not and cannot be a complete story because eventually communications between the family members faltered, and much remains unsaid. It was, after all, wartime; people don't say too much, even to each other. There are other relevant documents and letters in the wartime correspondence and diaries of Franciszka and Stefan, as well as a series of drawings by Franciszka called 'Unposted Letters', to be published soon by Gaberbocchus/De Harmonie in Amsterdam. There is much relevant material in the Themerson Archive, and several of the individuals who make an appearance here also have files there.

But, who am I? I've had several names, although the name I identify with is the only one I selected myself, my professional name: Jasia Reichardt. The name I was born with was Janina Chaykin [Jasia for short]; in 1942 it was changed to Maria

Janina Cegłowska; when I married Tony Richards in 1956, it was changed to Maria Richards; when I started writing about art in 1958, I changed it to Jasia Reichardt, the original surname of Tony's father. No more names. This one will do.

15 JOURNEYS WARSAW TO LONDON

15 JOURNEYS
WARSAW TO LONDON

We are in Warsaw. If we walk toward the park from the centre, it's not far. A five-minute walk down an elegant street full of trees. Facing the park entrance, we can stop. On the right is the building where I live: a large, solid, grey, nineteenth-century block of flats. Look up. On the first floor you see an iron balcony with pots of red geraniums. That's us. Now proceed through the large gate, into the courtyard with trees and flower-beds, avoiding the occasional bench and the wooden contraption for beating carpets. Turn left, and you'll find a door leading to a modest stone staircase of extreme greyness. Apartment numbers are listed outside; ours is number 12, on the first floor. There is no lift. Our door is on the right-hand side of the landing, and next to the doorbell is a nameplate, a nice bit of modernist typography: Seweryn Chaykin, architect/engineer. That's my father. We have arrived.

When the door opens, you are faced with three options.

First possibility. If you turn right you will walk into a little kitchen with a large window that gives onto the yard. You can open the window and shout to people below. I don't do that, or rather, it is not something I'm supposed to do. We are in a small, unremarkable kitchen. This is the domain of Marysia, our maid. I always imagine that she spends her time beating pieces of meat into pulp with a wooden mallet on a wooden block. The sound of the beating and the smell of raw meat wafts into the rest of the flat. Past the window, straight on, there is a door leading to somewhere beyond. I have never been through that door; it is private. The space into which this door leads belongs to Marysia. She is young, pretty, and short; perhaps the room beyond is small too.

Second possibility. There are two doors facing you when you enter the apartment. One slightly to the right and one slightly to the left. In between the two doors is a freestanding coat-rack. On top are hats, then looking down there are coats, then umbrellas, and finally galoshes, modestly confined to the floor. Having removed your outer garments, should you open the right-hand door you will see a basin on your right, a bath in front, and a tall round water heater to the left. Don't lean forward to look beyond the water heater. It is unwise, and you could just see something you'd rather not. You might encounter the unforgettable sight of an enormous naked pink bottom rising from the toilet seat. It is best to clear your throat as you enter, turn on the basin tap, and get on with washing your hands, if this is indeed what you want to do.

If after hanging up your coat you open the door on the left, you will see a normal sort of a lavatory with a wooden seat. To avoid frightening anyone who may be in the bathroom next door and looking accidentally beyond the water heater, it is best to sing.

Third possibility. If you turn left when the door of the apartment opens, you will enter the first in a sequence of three interconnected rooms. There is parquet floor throughout, and the colour of wood is the main colour of the apartment, except for the walls, which are white, or whitish. The first room is narrower than the others, but even before you can penetrate inside to examine its interior you will have to move around a heavy screen composed of three dark wooden frames on squat wooden legs. Inside the frames are three large two-sided oil paintings by Jakub Weinles. That's my grandfather. The paintings are of pink and white hollyhocks and other flowers on tall stems. The screen is heavy in weight and in colour. The colours are intense and dark. Do I like them? No, not really. These painted flowers are a natural part of my indoor world. They have always been there.

Looking past the screen, you see a window. It gives onto the street which has two names: Piękna (beautiful) and Piusa XI (in memory of Pope Pius XI). The street is lined with acacia and maple trees, and its cobblestones echo occasionally with the unmistakable sounds of horse-drawn carriages.

On the two walls to either side of the window are two long, built-in desks in dark wood, and above them are shelves with books. The desk on the left is where Sewek works in the evenings, and the one on the right belongs to Maryla (my mother); she sits there to draw. She makes illustrations for children's books. Her pictures are lovely, and, of course, I draw too.

Drawing by Maryla Weinles, 1925

White double doors lead to the next room, which is square, larger, and has multiple uses. The most imposing presence in the room is the Bechstein grand next to the French windows. Maryla is also a pianist. Maybe she is principally a pianist but also an illustrator, or is it the other way round? I don't know. She plays every day: Chopin, Schubert, Bach, Mozart, Beethoven. I sit under the piano and listen. One of the pieces I am particularly fond of is Schumann's *Papillons*, and that's what I ask for most often. The sound reverberates all through the entire space, and listening under the piano is one of my favourite things to do. Maryla's piano students come every day.

Illustrations by Maryla Weinles for *Żywe Literki* (Living Letters), 1928

One of the students is very familiar to me, Sewek's cousin, Zdzisław Libin, later Libera (below).

When the students arrive, I leave and go to another room. On the wall, to the right of the piano, and beneath an ugly, over-decorated, black and gold Chinese corner-shelf, is a glass-covered bookcase with art books. It is locked. I am allowed to take out some of the books, and I do spend a great deal of time looking at reproductions of paintings of girls in hats and decorative dresses, peasant scenes, landscapes. The most tantalising book, which I'm curious about but not allowed to look at, contains, as I later discover, the work of Aubrey Beardsley. On the other side of the room, opposite the French windows, is a cabinet containing glasses and a sideboard with lace napkins, tablecloths, and other things that accompany food. In front of this sideboard is a large wooden table. Visitors sit around this table, talk and eat, and talk and drink, and sometimes just sit and read. No, there are no sofas, settees, or easy chairs.

Now, you enter the last of the string of rooms, through a second set of double doors. Take care, my father's heavy leather-covered exercise rings hang on chains from the architrave between these doors. This last room is the bedroom. Opposite the doors is a double bed with an elaborately carved wooden frame. Next to it on the left, a large wardrobe with a mirror. It nearly fills the wall. On the right, between two windows, is Maryla's dressing table, also with a large mirror. Often, standing between the wardrobe and the dressing table, I try to catch some of the infinite number of reflections that always confound me. For a time I am convinced that if I try hard enough I shall succeed in seeing them all at once.

And now, for the most perfect piece of furniture ever made. It is on the right as you enter, past my bed. This perfection is my white cupboard, designed by Sewek. It has shelves, a wardrobe, drawers, cubby-holes, and a desk. It is an ideal model of cupboard-hood and my complete world. I don't use it quite as it is intended. On the shelves are decorations, small Chinese vases, miniature furniture, small shapes made of amber. On the desk is a cardboard model of a theatre. There are frequent performances in this theatre, sometimes with an audience, but usually without. My books (Andersen, the Brothers Grimm, Selma Lagerlöf, K. Czukowski, Janusz Korczak, Julian Tuwim) and collections of magazines for children are in my library under the desk.

Among the important magazines are *Małe Pisemko* (Little Magazine) and *Płomyk* (Flame), which includes many illustrations by Maryla and Franciszka, as well as stories by Stefan Themerson.

Two cover illustrations for children's magazines by Maryla Chaykin, 1930 and 1931

Some of the stories I know by heart. For instance the story of *Pan Tom buduje dom* written by Stefan and illustrated by Franciszka (*Mr Rouse Builds His House* in the English version). This story is presented in six tiny booklets in a box. To build a house is an enormous undertaking, involving as it does a great many choices, accidents, and problems. What kind of a house? Should it be a cottage on stilts? a pagoda? a house made of leaves? This saga, in its six miniature volumes, was the first book I read.

Stefan & Franciszka Themerson, *Pan Tom buduje dom*, 1938

Sometimes Maryla tells me stories. One unforgettable story is about the future, about a machine that can do everything by itself. It is a washing machine. You put in the laundry and it comes out clean and ironed. I am totally absorbed by it and am sure that one day I shall have just such a machine.

I am six.

By the way, my name is Janina Chaykin, Jasia for short. The year is 1939. It is early summer.

To go to school I wear a crimson crêpe blouse with long sleeves, a sailor's collar, a cravat tied in a bow, and a pleated navy blue skirt with braces. Dressing takes a long time. There are many flaps and buttons. I attend a French pre-school and I hate it. I'm frightened of being among strangers, never mind the language. My mother takes me for a walk in Łazienki Park on the way to school. She explains that I'll get used to the school and the language; that French is important because one day I shall live in France. She promises that when she picks me up in the afternoon we'll go straight to a book and stationery shop and she will buy me a present. I collect 'malowanki' (embossed coloured pictures of angels, animals, and flowers, printed on large sheets from which they can be cut out and sold singly), wrapping papers, and books. We go there practically every day. I am a collector of objects made of paper. Quantity matters. When asked whether I'd prefer four hardback volumes of Hans Christian Andersen or six in paperback, I choose the latter. Sometimes I manage to avoid school—a headache, stomach-ache, or some other ache that allows me to manipulate the situation. Gradually school is accepted, friends are made, and I even learn to repeat one or two jokes in French which I don't understand myself but which, to my surprise and gratification, make grown-ups laugh.

Apart from school, there are lessons of a different sort, and these somehow I don't forget. Of course, I don't think of them as lessons, but that is indeed what they are. Lesson no. 1. In the dentist's waiting room, I sit trembling with anticipation holding my mother's hand. Opposite, a little boy younger than me is crying his eyes out. My mother tells me to go and console him. This is what I do. He stops crying, and I stop being nervous. Lesson no. 2. Collecting conkers with a friend from school. Sewek is sitting on a branch shaking them down but most of them fall near my school-friend and fewer near me. We take her home, and when I'm alone with my parents I ask them why she was getting more conkers than me. 'She's our guest', they explain.

Lesson no. 3. Giving away toys. All those that I no longer play with are put in a basket and I go with my mother to a children's ward in a psychiatric hospital to distribute them among the patients. The toys are happily parted with and gratefully received. Before we leave I also notice that on a table there are some small figurines made out of bread and I desperately want one of them: a small horse. I am not allowed to take it. Giving away something unwanted does not mean that I can take something in return. Later, at home, I decide to make my own horse out of bread.

Occasionally when I am told to do or not to do something which doesn't make sense to me, I protest. When I am told not to play with the gatekeeper's daughter, I am upset. Many years later I learn that the gatekeeper was untrustworthy and that my mother was protecting me from the possibility of being the subject of some unpleasant anti-Semitic jibes. Of course, at the time I have no idea that I am Jewish, nor that anybody could or would discriminate against me.

My life is quiet and pleasant. I have a teddy bear called Sebastian given to me by my aunt and uncle, Franciszka and Stefan Themerson. They actually wanted to give me a tailless Manx cat but my mother said that she couldn't cope with an animal in the flat. I am happy with Sebastian, as well as with my large collection of cards, games, and publications, most featuring illustrations by Franciszka and Maryla, and stories by Stefan. I have many things to play with and to amuse me, but what I desire most deeply is a doll with grey hair plaited and rolled around her ears, from a toy-shop called Malanowski on the street called Marszałkowska. I can have the doll as a reward for walking down the stairs from our apartment by myself. Marysia will meet me in the courtyard. I am an abject coward, and try as I may, I cannot go through with it. An unspeakable fear seems to lodge itself in my stomach. I cannot walk down the stairs by myself, and I have to give up my dream doll.

At the age of six, I have two problems. Problem no. 1 remains a fear of going anywhere by myself. Problem no. 2 is a very different matter. It is my hair. It has never been cut since I was born, it is long and thick, and I am unable to deal with it. I cannot comb it or plait it by myself. It becomes the stuff of my nightmares.

'She's being brought up in cotton-wool', says our cousin Ludka. 'She is a genius', says my father. My mother doesn't comment, but she too anticipates a brilliant future for me.

What does my mother look like? She looks lovely. She has long dark brown hair which she wears in a bun, and she has blue eyes. She is short-sighted and wears glasses. What else do I remember? I can still see her orange powder puff and the gold and orange art nouveau powder box on the dressing table, and I also see that as a rule her dresses have a great many cloth-covered buttons running down her back. Her favourite flower is the narcissus. What I remember with the greatest clarity are her intricate illustrations for children's books, and my favourite pieces of Chopin and Schubert, which she plays for me whenever I ask her.

I call my father by his first name, Sewek. He has curly hair and brown eyes, and he laughs a lot. He is of medium height. He plays the piano too. Maryla told me that when he has two drinks he speaks French; after a third, it's Latin. He is a thoughtful, kind person. He delayed his architectural studies for several years to take a job and support his two younger brothers, Michał and Paweł, during their years at college. Both of them will become lawyers. Sewek works for TOR (Towarzystwo Osiedli Robotniczych), the Society for Social Housing, which in 1935 in the Warsaw district of Koło starts to build modest family houses and blocks of flats. By 1939, this new housing is occupied by 4,500 people. Social housing is something new and enormously popular. The interiors are modest and simple: there are built-in cupboards and communal washing and drying machines. The head of TOR is Roman Piotrowski. The owner of TOR, Jerzy Michałowski, another of Sewek's colleagues, is also a close friend of the Themersons.

Jerzy Michałowski, identity document

Sewek Chaykin with colleague Halina
Pągowska on the building site of Koło,
Warsaw, c. 1937

Sewek Chaykin, on the left, with
two colleagues, in front of the social
housing buildings in Koło, 1938

When Sewek comes home from work, he puts on his casual jacket (called a 'bonżurka') and then carefully examines the pile of books and various objects I have assembled into a precarious pile on the floor for him to look at. Yes, he says that I am going to be an architect, I am nearly an architect already. I agree. Yes of course, I shall be an architect.

Visits to family are frequent. My maternal grandparents live not far from us on ulica Królewska. My grandfather, Jakub Weinles, is a much-admired painter of people, interiors, landscapes, and scenes from Jewish life. I like his studio and become very fond of the smell of oil paint. It is the room in their house that I go into first, to look at the paintings—or rather to look at one particular painting, the portrait of Franciszka aged two. It becomes a ritual that, as soon as I arrive, I kiss this painting, which is placed on the floor, leaning against an easel, so that I can reach it. My grandmother Łucja's piano is also in this large bright room. It is an upright piano with gilt candle-holders on either side. She too plays a classical repertoire.

Painting by Jakub Weinles of Łucja and Maryla at the piano, 1907

Łucja gives piano lessons and taught both Maryla and Franciszka before they entered the conservatoire, followed by the Academy of Fine Art. Franciszka eventually concentrates on art; Maryla pursues both. The sitting room has a very different atmosphere from grandfather's studio: it is dark and warm with heavy drapery and thick rugs. Everyone sits around the large oval table, reading, talking, and drawing.

Painting by Jakub Weinles of the balcony on ulica Królewska,
1930

The height of the large hanging lamp can be adjusted and is raised for meals. And then the maid clears the table and covers it with a starched white damask tablecloth. The only daylight in this room comes from the French window that leads onto a very small balcony overlooking the courtyard. The balcony is crowded with plants. There is a table and a chair but I've not seen anyone sit on it. You can see it in my grandfather's painting.

On the same floor, on the other side of the hall, lives my great-grandmother. I avoid visiting her because old people frighten me. Even so, I am quite prepared to accept the presents that await me when I do manage to visit, and one of my favourite toys is the green wind-up frog which can jump and which I carry away from her flat in triumph.

My most enjoyable visits are to the Themersons. Before they leave for Paris in 1938, they live in a studio flat on the top floor of a new block on ulica Czeczota, on the outskirts of Warsaw. Their home is the antithesis of my grandparents' house. It is in a modern building, with a concrete staircase and a rooftop ter-race. The studio is large and light and furnished with a large table and wicker furniture. There is also a desk with pyramids of books. It is on that desk that Stefan introduces me to three-dimensional illustrations. The illegible illustrations printed in a chaos of red and green come to life as I put on red and green glasses. There is always something new to see. Together we make a kaleidoscope. I am given a stereo-viewer for looking at stere-oscopic photographs. I am introduced to paper engineering. But my greatest interest is directed toward their Siamese cat, Anastasia, and her kittens.

Drawing by Franciszka Themerson, 1935

The Themersons' books, written by Stefan and illustrated by Franciszka, are the first books I read. There are a dozen or so, all about the wonders of the world around me: the magic of electricity, magnetism, time, the post office, words, the alphabet. There are no mermaids, no angels or witches, no Aladdins, just what we can see, use, and touch.

Summers are spent in my grandparents' villa in Falenica. It is a wooden bungalow with a surrounding veranda. It isn't far from Warsaw, perhaps an hour by train, and is situated in the middle of a wood. My mother and I spend two or three months there every year. My father arrives at the weekends, and so do other visitors, uncles and cousins, and we play cards and other games. I have a bow and arrow which makes me feel grown-up, and I strut about the wood wondering what to shoot at. French lessons continue. Maryla has decided, and I agree with alacrity, that once my secondary education is completed I shall join Franciszka and Stefan in Paris and will study at the Sorbonne. And so my future is decided. Much to my relief it is still far enough away that I don't have to worry yet about being separated from my mother.

•

Do I know in advance that the war is imminent? I am not sure. I do know on the 1st of September 1939, the first day of the war, that we are under attack: bombs fall on Warsaw and my mother and I rush into a shelter. There are no special shelters. There are simply cellars, and most buildings have them. As we run down, we see the sky in flames. Around us everything seems to be burning but what is worse than the actual fire is the sound of the descending planes. The sirens make the most frightening noise I've ever heard. I keep wondering if the building will fall on top of us. On the 1st of September my normal life ends and what starts is as unimaginable as it is hard to describe. For the first time I recognise that my world is no longer a secure place. This is the end of plans for my future, the end of any plans at all.

Warsaw surrenders on the 28th of September, but new dangers emerge day by day. After that explosive beginning events come into focus slowly. Life is like a chain along which one moves from one link to the next. I live in the present, through minutes and hours, perhaps not even days. It is difficult to imagine what any tomorrow could be like.

Sewek is not around. He is in Lwów with his brothers and the other men who were neither too young nor too old to fight. He sends this telegram: 'the families are well', to Franciszka and Stefan in France, c/o the Polish Embassy in Paris, on the 22nd of November.

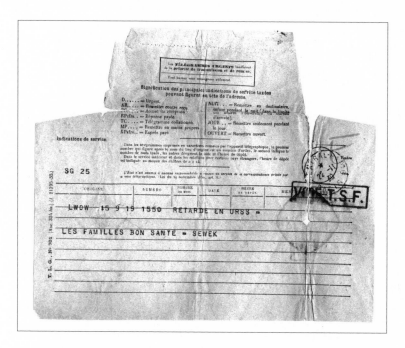

At this time, the Themersons are still in Paris. However, soon enough, Franciszka will escape to London, by ship from Bayonne, with other members of the Polish government-in-exile, while Stefan, whose infantry regiment will have disbanded in Brittany, will walk to Paris and eventually find shelter with the Polish Red Cross in Voiron. They will be reunited in London in the summer of 1942.

Meanwhile, our flat in ulica Piusa fills with relatives who lost their homes during the bombing. The most important person to move in with us is my grandmother, Łucja Weinles. The Wein-leses' flat, including my grandfather's studio, burns down on the first day of the war. All the paintings are lost. All of them, including my favourite portrait of Franciszka aged two. Another picture that is so familiar to me is also lost, the pastel portrait of my mother as a young girl of about ten, with long plaits and a green butterfly net against a forest background. This was hanging in the main room. And, of course, all the other paintings are lost in flames as well: portraits, paintings of flowers and landscapes, sad paintings of bearded men in black, of beggars with toys, monkeys, and music boxes, of people running and standing and looking. These last paintings had been too grim, too sad for my taste. I had last seen them all together on the walls of a gallery, at my grandfather's memorial exhibition in September 1938, after his death earlier that year. The subjects of many of those paintings were the rituals and scenes of Jewish life. My first visit to an art exhibition. The exhibition was just too sad. The people around me wore too much black; I preferred to think of my grandfather's studio with its few familiar portraits in light colours. It was on that bleak day that my father promised to take me to a film starring Shirley Temple. We went to the cinema together and the day changed its mood. I love Shirley Temple! Perhaps, perhaps, one day I too could have short hair with curls?

Now I am spending all my time with adults. I sleep in a gap between two beds. On one side is an aged grand-uncle, Władek Kaufman, grandmother Łucja's brother, and on the other his friend, Ginia. Between the air raids, I sit and read. The windows of the flat are shattered, glass is everywhere, and the cold is un-thinkable. Like Siberia, says my mother. The windows are now covered with blackout cloth. I am wearing a coat, scarf, hat, and woollen tights, and I sit as close as I can to the white tiled stove in the corner of the room.

The most spectacular fire at the end of our street consumes the building of the famous chocolatier, E. Wedel. I think about the chocolates, the cakes, the sweets going up in smoke. The cus-tard tarts I used to buy. Ask for 'the well-baked ones', Maryla used to say. E. Wedel burns for two days and on the third day there is just blue-grey smoke surrounding a bare grey ruin. On the street I find a small jug of fluted pink glass with two gold bands. Could I take it? I wonder, and am pleasantly surprised when my mother says that I can keep it.

Three activities permeate my daily life, whose strangeness becomes normal. I read, draw, and do school work. I don't ask questions because I can see that they upset my mother. Nobody makes plans or talks about the future. I am surrounded by adults who are obviously preoccupied with insurmountable problems. But they care for me and that is enough.

•

And here, until the summer of 1942, my memories will be inter-spersed with Maryla's and Łucja's letters to Franciszka Themer-son in Paris and later in London, travelling as they do halfway round Europe to reach their destination. While I am still with my mother, I don't understand anything about these letters, even though I add an occasional paragraph or a drawing.

23

I shall look at this correspondence with enormous hesitation and pain, fifty years later in London, and wonder endlessly at all the random events and the chances that made it possible for me to survive to tell this story.

You are lucky, said Franciszka.

•

Franciszka is Maryla's younger sister by seven years. In 1931, she marries Stefan Themerson, writer, experimental film-maker, and author of children's books; together they produce a number of avant-garde films in Warsaw during the 1930s. Their move from Warsaw to Paris in 1938 is to fulfil a wish to be at the centre of the art world.

The Themersons in Paris in their studio in Arcueil, 1938

It is there that, when I am old enough, I am to join them in order to study at the Sorbonne. In the event, war upsets all our plans. The Themersons find their way to London, where from 1942 on they continue their work in film, art, and books. And so it is in London rather than in Paris that I eventually join them.

Most of Maryla's and Łucja's letters to Franciszka tell or hint at the story of the two years of our life spent principally in the Warsaw ghetto. The letters pass through the careful scrutiny of the censor, who marks them with numbers. Some parts of the letters are excised. Maryla and Łucja use a code, but there is no pattern to what might or might not be censored, and this paired with their precautions make some of the letters difficult to unravel. But there are other reasons beside censorship not to go into very much detail. They don't want to upset Franciszka, and so they avoid revealing more than is absolutely necessary. It is also vital that some of the people mentioned should not be identified. Names are changed or slightly altered. Sometimes, individuals are referred to by their relationship to the writers rather than by name.

In all there are fifteen letters and thirty-one postcards. There may have been more letters which failed to reach their destination. Their route is through Bucharest, Antwerp, and later, through Lisbon. Once we are in the ghetto, they are posted outside by friends and acquaintances.

The mood of the letters changes almost imperceptibly as one reads through them. At first, there are optimistic moments.

Later, even though both Łucja and Maryla are anxious not to reveal everything about their situation, it becomes obvious that matters are going from bad to worse.

•

I have decided not to edit the letters and postcards despite some repetition. Each letter, whatever its content, is primarily proof that the writer is, or was at the time of writing, still alive. The letters have their own texture and pattern. The entire correspondence resembles a chain-stitch that goes back over itself, progressing slowly. With every stitch there is a small change, a new item of information, a nuance of mood that casts increasingly dark shadows. The letters start on an even note, but gradually reveal growing despair. And then they stop. They are written over a period of two and a half years. The last postcard is dated 20 June 1942.

•

Franciszka, meanwhile, is well aware of the events in Warsaw. She works as a cartographer for the Polish government-in-exile and illustrates the wartime pamphlets they publish; news from Poland percolates straight through to their office, first in Angers and then, after June 1940, at the Ministry of Information and Documentation at Stratton House near London's Green Park.

Letter from Maryla to Franciszka in Paris:

24 February 1940

Darling Franeczko

A while ago I sent you a card and a letter from our mother and Stefek's, via Bucharest. You already know that mother and Jasia are in Otwock. They went for a visit and this is their third week. I am in Warsaw with Stach and Wisia. I am glad that you already have Sewek's address. Do write to him. He is working together with his brothers and Halina, he misses us very much but his situation is not bad. Stefek's mother, Irka, Stefan and Anka are well. You probably received detailed information directly from them. Don't send any money darling, there is no shortage, and besides it is pointless because to date mother hasn't received any. I am in my own apartment, on Piusa XI. My mother-in-law, Stach, Władek, Lutek, Cela (Adolf died), Gucia—are no longer at home. The family of Heniek has two rooms. I am happy that you are working and managing. I dream of seeing you as soon as possible. Mother is brave, keeps well—even though all of father's paintings are lost, even his bronze palette. Jasia is doing school-work, she is following a 2nd year course with her mother. For her and for Wisia there is no school . . . she draws very well. When she returns from Zofiówka, both she and Wisia will be learning to play the piano. The grand piano is still here (not everyone has . . .) And I also feel well, although it is cold and difficult. In October Jasia had scarlet fever, but lightly and without complications. Despite the inspection from the sanitary office—she was in bed, anyway there was already glass in the windows . . . We live for letters from our nearest and dearest. Today is the first day of spring, 5° above zero, if only this temperature would hold. For whole weeks it stayed around -20°. Despite this—we haven't had a day without coal and without making a fire in the stove. Anyway, there is water, light and gas—so now life is not too difficult. Write often, lots of kisses. Maryla

This letter to Franciszka is sent via Hania Kawa in Bucharest, a distant cousin. Maryla adds a note to her:

Dear Hania Kawa, thank you so much for the opportunity to send a letter to Franka. Please be so kind as to write a few words to Sewek, Hołówki 23—he would certainly be very glad. I do hope that for you time is passing without trauma and distress. I send you my kindest regards and ask that you send Franka some news about yourself.
Maryla Chaykin

Hania Kawa keeps in touch with the Themersons. She acts as a central post office for a great number of friends and relations. The personal news she sends this time is only that her own mother lost her life in the Warsaw bombing.

Ill with scarlet fever, I spend two or three weeks in bed. Apart from my mother's constant care, three things become central to me. I have two volumes of the magazines *Jugend* and *Fliegende Blätter*, which I look at. I can't read German but I have a passion for looking at pictures. I also have Lola, a Dresden china doll which I am allowed to sleep with when I am ill. Maryla feeds me with mashed apple, white cheese, and kogel mogel (egg yolks beaten with sugar).

I don't remember the visit to Zofiówka, in Otwock, the psychiatric hospital in the beautiful grounds that Maryla mentions in her letter, but I went there on many occasions; it was effectively another family home. Zofiówka was directed by two doctors, Stefan Themerson's sister Irena and her husband, Stefan Miller.

Different people move into our flat. Now it is Uncle Stach, Sewek's oldest brother, my paternal grandmother, Cecylia, and Stach's daughter, Wisia. She is a few years older than me, has a single plait, and is beautiful. I have two plaits, not so elegant and not so grown-up. I want to be like her.

The new memorable events are inoculations against typhus, ration coupons, and the introduction of arm bands with the Star of David. These become compulsory on the 23rd of November 1939. They are made of plastic and connected with a piece of elastic. The Star of David is blue, the background white. The armbands are intrusive and crude. The size is specified. I offer to embroider one for my mother—she shouldn't have to wear plastic. I have a white piece of cloth and make a Star of David in chain-stitch. Perhaps the thin lines of the star do not quite conform to the regulated size. I am too young to wear the armband, not yet ten, but would like to, to be just like my mother and other members of my family. But in the street, people's armbands are obscured by coats, bags, scarves. Perhaps I won't bother with the armband after all.

New prohibitions and orders come thick and fast. After July 1940, Jews are not allowed to change residence without written permission of the local authorities; cannot leave their homes between 9 A.M. and 5 P.M. without a permit; cannot employ non-Jews; cannot enter parks, walk down streets perpendicular to Aleje Ujazdowskie, enter various squares, sit on public benches in town. There are also other prohibitions, including: no riding in taxis, no carrying of briefcases, no wearing felt hats, no participating in athletic events, no making calls from telephone booths, no having gold tooth fillings.

I now know that I am Jewish. I am not quite sure what that is. Nobody explains to me what it means to be Jewish. 'Do we have to be Jewish?' I ask my mother, hopefully, 'couldn't we be something else?'—but this appears not to be a matter of choice, and from what I see around me, being Jewish seems not to be a good thing.

Letter from Łucja and Maryla, with a note from me to Franciszka and Stefan:

11 March 1940

My dearest ones! Not long ago I wrote a letter to you my dears together with the others in Otwock. Many times Stefan and Irenka invited me to their home, and since I was anxious that Jasia should spend a little time in the country, I went there with her in February. We returned on Sunday, 3rd March. The child improved a lot because she spent several hours a day in the open air despite the great freeze. Apparently I also improved a great deal, but as usually happens after a few days, I forgot that I was in the country. There, everything is all right, they are well. For the time being one can get everything. At that time there were also Anka and Stefek's mother, who looks well and for the time being has no intention of returning to Warsaw. The apartment on Złota is also damaged a bit, especially the rooms that give onto the courtyard. For the moment they are not rebuilding but all the furniture is intact. Władek is also there, he works a bit in the office. He also has no reason to return to Warsaw because his apartment and his possessions were burnt. About our apartment, as I see from your letters, you already know. Now I very much regret Franuś that you didn't take with you a few pictures, because there is nothing left. [But] that could not, and cannot, be helped.

We live together with Maryla and Jasia, and a month ago Stach and Wisia moved in with us and it is pleasanter for us to be together. We have enough for our modest needs and I was very distressed that you sent us some money and anyway it may not arrive and it would be good if it was returned and don't do this anymore, don't send anything please, I am happy that I have news from you that you work and I am sure very hard and a great deal, in order to be able to survive somehow.

Recently several cards arrived from you and even those sent a long time ago. We also write very often. If you have the opportunity to write another letter, let us know a bit more what you are working on, if the books you illustrated in August came out, and generally how you live, if you meet friends. Of those close to us, the Hallers live where they lived before, they are in good health, also Wandzia and Jaś. Adolf died on the 11th October, Lutek with his wife and mother are in Białystok and Olek in Vilnius. During the last few days we received a card from Sewek, he is well and is working.

[paragraph crossed out by the censor]

~~Lola, Ania's mother, who sewed your underwear asks if you would communicate with a woman, whose address I am sending you. She is, I understand, very nice. Let her know that Lola and Rózia are well. To her aunt~~

[and there follow a couple of additional lines cut out by the censor]

~~tell her that Rózia and the children are with Sewek.~~

My dearest ones, I embrace you and kiss you many times, be well and happy.

Yours Ł.W.

from Maryla:

My dearest ones

You already know from mother about the most important things. That we are well and in good spirits. For us the real satisfaction is the thought that you live in more or less normal conditions. The sphere of our interests is very small. Ration cards, typhus inoculation, armbands with the star of Zion and other little aches.

Despite this, Jasia and Wisia grow, learn and it seems that our present times don't leave any traces—at any rate that is what we are trying to achieve. Both of them practise scales and exercises, write dictations and do homework. We live with Stach [words cut out] . . . Mother in law and Marysia will probably move in with us . . . [words cut out] but cheerful!

Write to us often, dearest, how is everything with you? Do you walk about town at 8 in the evening? Are cinemas and parks open to everyone? It will be a pleasure to even read about it. I kiss you, Maryla

[And an addition from me:]
Dearest Franka and Stefek

I was in Otwock and had very good time. I am preparing for the third form. 2000 kisses. Jasia

Letter from Maryla to Franciszka:

5 April 1940

Dear Franeczko, thank you for the birthday wishes. Now that there is neither Father nor the old house, and you are far away—I am constantly reminded of the birthdays fragrant with hyacinths from those years long ago. One can hardly believe that fewer than 100 years elapsed since that time. I am pleased that Stefanek is with you. Surely he won't go to school since he is so short-sighted. It is horrid that such a big lad apes Radwanicha, but probably not the one from old pre-war times. Hania Kawa wrote to me about your work. We are all quite well. Janka went through a bout of scarlet fever in October, in a mild form. Since there were many people here and few beds, I slept with her in one bed for two nights, before I realised that the rash looked rather like scarlet fever. I had a very good doctor. Janka was sitting with poultices round her neck and ears (just in case), every few days a diagnosis was made, she drank milk and ate apples. After six weeks she got up healthy and without complications. For six weeks I paraded in a cap and a white overall, in the room, apart from beds, there was only a basin with [chemical vapour]; on the door was a notice: entrance forbidden, (this was ordered by the sanitary doctor). And in reality not even a lame dog not a soul appeared throughout that time. During that time we had neither pleasant visits, nor unwelcome ones, whereas afterwards there was no shortage of visits . . . When Jasia got ill I already had single windowpanes mounted in the frames. I lugged them with Kazia from Próżna Street. In all my life I have never carried

anything quite so heavy. After a week I got a glazier, and after two weeks window putty. When Jasia was in bed I thought that it might be necessary to change the apartment and already enquired about the price of an ambulance and looked for a place to store the piano. Grandmother went away before Janka got ill, but it wasn't even necessary, but she didn't have her things and there was a likelihood of a hard winter. In September I went to visit Ludka [Haller Sobieralska]. I only found Wandzia, I was there for quite a long time, and then we left together. Immediately after our departure, their 4 rooms were turned into two. Also during that time, for a short while, we exchanged our flat, and had a large room, not so light but spacious, three floors below our current apartment [i.e., the cellar]. There were very many of us, it was very jolly especially because there was a lot of singing...
One of the neighbours let it be known that the engineer's wife [i.e., Maryla] doesn't have an apartment for the time being—this was a female dentist. After a few days relatives and friends started arriving—they were looking for Mother. Lutek had to go to live with his parents, after he carried his father in a wheel barrow to my Mother, but they missed each other and he went to Luchna, where Adolf spent the night in the yard. After a week they returned to their own place and once more Adolf left—in a cart. Lusia came to visit me recently, Olek's wife. Because she thought that she might be changing her apartment, I wanted to take Father's things to my place. I went, but too late. The flat was sublet, the things stayed behind... Recently, I met Sewek's neighbours. He's had enough of his present flat and would like to take over the old one. He would wait until it gets warmer

35

and the flat will be renovated. I am sad about this, but what can one do, perhaps he will still change his mind. As far as my birthday is concerned, as you know, I have reached a significant round number [40]. What terrible luck! Perhaps there will be jobs for unemployed women (Irka does not come into this category), washing, cleaning, etc.—and now it is already a foregone conclusion that I won't be allowed to work. If only I was born six months later!!! You also asked about Lutek, he is with Sewek. He went with his mother, wife in 9th month of pregnancy and everything. The things they lost—and they arrived with the child. My mother-in-law lives with Michał's in-laws, before the move she was in her bathroom. It is a very good and pleasant bathroom, it is still there. Today, Mother is starting to give lessons at Ada's. I am very happy about it, not only for the sake of the income, because until now she has been too preoccupied with work in the house. Kazia [the maid] has been dispensed with, and Stach's Helenka got a job at the treasury office. Janka is learning to play the piano. I am also playing. Every few days I organise for myself a little farewell concert. Because one never knows. Perhaps I'll sell the instrument, or give it to the poor . . . Well, that's enough for today. Write darlings.

I kiss you, Maryla

Mother didn't get your letter . . . don't worry, we don't lack anything.

Kisses and embraces my darlings. Another time I'll write more. Your Ł.W.

Maryla mentions hyacinths which I remember standing in a clay pot on the dining room table on her birthday on April 16th. They are blue, always blue. In their wartime correspondence Franciszka and Stefan also write about hyacinths, which they buy for themselves as a present from the other. But why hyacinths, since Maryla's favourite flowers are narcissi?

I don't always know who the people are to whom Maryla refers. I surmise that "Radwanicha," an unflattering change to Mrs Radwan's surname, is someone connected with Maryla's work as illustrator of children's books.

Card from Irena Furstenberg at 37 Colonielaan, Antwerp, to Stefan Themerson at 37 Quai des Grands Augustins, Paris 6:

17 June 1940

My dearest, today we received your card Franuś, and before that a letter from Hania. We are very happy when we receive any news. I kiss you many times. Ł.W.

[in Łucja's handwriting, though signed with Maryla's name]

Dear Franeczko, thank you for the birthday wishes. And I wish you the same. We are all in good health. Jasia benefited greatly from her stay in Zofiówka. Mother is healthy, brave and calm. We are managing, we don't lack anything. Sewek decided to occupy the same flat as before the war. I expect that soon you will receive a letter from me—with a line from him. I wrote two extensive letters recently through Hania, however I doubt that they reached you. I would like to be assured that you are all right. It's probably very expensive where you are and it is probably very difficult for you. Stach's acquaintance, whom you met, I suppose, told you a little about us. The main thing is that it's spring, the frosts have gone and the mood is improving—a bit more and it will be well. I kiss you heartily. Soon, I'll write again.

Maryla

Letter from Maryla to Franciszka:

11 October 1940

Dear Franeczko, thank you for the letter and news about your health, both of you; if only everything could be all right now! Beginning with 28th June, the first telegram to Hania, we had frequent news from her about your search [Franciszka is looking for Stefan who has joined a Polish regiment in France, which then disbands in Brittany, after which he proceeds to Paris by foot], I can just imagine what you went through. A few weeks before receiving your letter we had some reassuring news from Hania . . .

My dear, how do you live in that maelstrom, you must surely have many friends who somehow make your life easier. Does Stefek write often? Sewek hasn't changed his address so far, which I am glad about. He wrote to you c/o [Urszula] Lubelska's first address. We are all in good health, in good spirits, and we dream about being together with Sewek and both of you. Apart from Stach and Wisia, Maryla's mother-in-law is living with us. Grandmother got rather ill during the summer and on the 7th of July there was her funeral in Otwock . . . Mother has a few students. Janka is taking lessons from me, together with another girl. She is going through the 3rd form. She is healthy and grown-up, even though we didn't go away in the summer, and only went for walks in the streets. Mr Bech[stein] rented a room at Wandzia's. Jasia goes to play the piano at a friend's house. We would be really happy if you could manage from time to time to send us some information about yourself. Don't worry about us, we are in good health and don't lack anything.

Lots of kisses—Maryla

Stefek's family, Heniek, Władek, Ginia—all are well.

Address letters to me to Piusa XI.

My darling Franuś. Your last handwritten letter of 8th August made me very happy. I carry it with me and read it all the time. I can't imagine at all how you live now that your circumstances are so different. Can you communicate with Stefek, and where is he now, what is he doing, how is he? And you my darling how are you, how is your health? You write, 'fine', as usual, but this doesn't tell me anything. Write again a bit more, are you working and how do you live? We live together with the whole family, that is Maryla with Jasia, me, also Mrs Ch[ajkin], Stach and Wisia. For the time being we are still on ulica Piusa XI, perhaps it will be possible to remain here. With Irenka all is as before. Stefek's mother is together with them, and Anka is in Warsaw, but visits them often. Władek also works there, and Ginia in Warsaw, in an office. I kiss and hug you many times, my darling. I am very grateful to you for news, because anxiety is very distressing; I also always try to reply at once, but I don't know if you have received anything.

Again, a lot of kisses from your very loving Ł.W.

If you are able to write to Stefek send him kisses, hugs and warm greetings from me.

When we move to the ghetto in October 1940, the white cupboard goes with us. Nothing much else that I recall, except the Dresden china doll, Lola. I don't remember the details of the move. The furniture is loaded onto a large horse-cart. There is the dining room table and chairs, my cupboard, a palm in a pot, but not a single mirror. Once more we live on a street with two names, but our official address is Śliska 7, flat no. 10. On the other side of the block is ulica Sienna. And once more we are on the first floor. There are many acquaintances on the block. There are friends and relatives down the street. My mother says it's a village. Our flat has three rooms.

As you enter through the front door, the first door on the left is a small bathroom with a lavatory. There is nothing strange about this bathroom. I go in there often. For some reason I've taken to rushing in and washing my hands several times a day, perhaps for something to do. The second door on the left is the kitchen. I don't go in there. It is occupied mostly by my two grandmothers and Ludka Haller Sobieralska, the three senior ladies in the apartment, who do whatever cooking is to be done.

As you enter the front door, the first door on the right leads to the biggest room. In it lives my grandmother no. 2, Cecylia

[Cesia] Chajkin, her son, Stach, my father's older brother, and his daughter Wisia. Stach is a cellist but he doesn't play now. And there is my beautiful cousin, Wisia, a few years older than me.

The second door on the right leads to our room, Maryla's, my grandmother Łucja's, and mine. Entrance to the third room is through our room and so our room is a sort of corridor. In the third room live Henryk (Heniek) Haller Sobieralski, his wife Ludwika (Ludka), and their daughter Wanda (Wandzia).

Our room has two French windows with a balcony giving onto ulica Sienna, but there is a dark 3.5 metre wall just outside and little else, no trees, nothing. There is something on top of the wall. I think it's glass. In our room, there are three beds, one against each of the empty walls of the room. There is also a metal bed, which is folded into a very high box. It stands between the two French windows and is covered alternately with a pale blue or pale green crocheted shawl. The texture is rough, the colour insipid, but this uneven surface is now my nest. My white cupboard is next to the window on the right. In the cubby holes are three bags of cereal. In the centre of the room there is a table and several chairs. I think that is all. Maryla mentions a palm in her letters but I don't remember it. During the following two years I spend a great deal of time perched on top of the high box with two or three atlases. I look through them endlessly and with considerable pleasure. Now Africa is my favourite continent. Perhaps because it is so obviously distant—a warm and exotic elsewhere.

Card from Maryla to Franciszka, posted by Maria Tywonek, Marszałkowska 94, Warsaw, to F. Themerson, Box 506, Lisbon, Portugal, received by Lisbon post office 29 November 1940:

7 November 1940

> Dear Franeczko, not so long ago I sent you a letter. Today, I received a card from Hania [Kawa] about you and Stefek. I am sending her your address, perhaps she will be able to send it to Stefek. Darling, we are all in good health, we worry about you, and worry that you and Stefek are separated. Sewek is where he was from the beginning. Mother is giving lessons, I also. Sewek helps us out a bit. We live on Śliska 7/10. We changed flats. We have three rooms with a kitchen and live with my mother-in-law, Stach, and Heniek; they are no better off than we are. We have a better flat than before and everything is falling into place satisfactorily.
>
> I kiss you a lot—Maryla
>
> I kiss you and embrace you many times my darling, Ł.W.

On the 16th of November, the ghetto is sealed off. I'm not sure if I am aware of it. Things happen quite gradually. I don't know where Sewek is and I wonder when we shall see him, but I don't ask. I'm sure that I'll be told when the time comes. We don't talk about the future and don't make plans except about my schoolwork.

Card from Łucja to Franciszka, posted by Maria Tywonek, Marszałkowska 94, Warsaw, to F. Themerson, Box 506, Lisbon, Portugal:

18 November 1940

My darling Franuś

It is already a long time since I had news of you. Darling, write a few words. I had a letter from Hania [Kawa], she wrote me about Stefek, apparently he wrote to her himself. We have changed our apartment. We have three very nice rooms, sunny, on the first floor. Stach lives with us, as well as his mother and Wisia, also Wandzia with her parents. We are in good health and have enough for our modest needs. I work a little bit and Jasia is doing school work in a group, with Maryla. What are you doing my darling, do you have a bit of work, and how is your health. We have news from Sewek, he helps us a bit. Irenka with her husband and mother are and work where they were before. I kiss and embrace you many times. Ł.W.

Card from Maria Chaykin, Śliska 7, m. 10, Warsaw, to Halina Pągowska, ulica Bolecha 24, Koło, Warsaw:

20 November 1940

Dear Halina, would you be so kind as to buy me a large pregnant female rabbit that will have little ones very quickly. If you could also buy me a kilo of fresh butter and two kilos of semolina, I would be very grateful and pay you back with thanks. If you could do this for me—please if possible before Sunday.

Warm greetings from Maria Chaykin

Maryla takes me for walks. Up and down our street and around the block, and again around the block. Soon after our arrival we sometimes visit a local garden. There, a group of children plays games, reads aloud, and sings. I do my best to join in. The teacher sings part of a song and each child in turn is asked to repeat it. 'Who will go first?' asks the teacher. Immediately, I raise my hand, am led into the middle of the circle and burst forth, with impressive volume and expression but completely out of tune. I get a prize—for courage. Musically, I have little talent. Considering that every member of my family plays at least one instrument, I am something of an anomaly. Maryla has been teaching me to play the piano since the age of four, but without much success. She takes me to a central hall where there is a piano to continue my lessons. I don't like the piano: it's an upright. The janitor passing by, hearing my desperate efforts, calls out: 'Rome wasn't built in a day!' This is my last piano lesson in Poland. The building where this memorable lesson takes place is a soup kitchen. It is a palace of sorts with an enormous spiral marble staircase. I have vertigo and descend the stairs on all fours.

Sometimes when I go for a walk with Maryla, we stop and take a different route. She doesn't explain and I don't ask. Eventually we take our walks on our street only, to the end and back, to the end and back.

Maryla teaches me to draw: the relationship between the nose and the ear; folded arms; kneeling posture; walking and running legs. One day she also makes a drawing for me of two naked children. 'This is a girl' and 'this is a boy'; apart from noticing the boy's extra feature I am reassured that the girl has nice long curls.

Letter from Maryla to Franciszka:

24 November 1940

Dear Franeczko, a few days ago, Mother sent you a card. Today, however, a letter came to us from you for Heniek and his family, and so I am writing again. We changed our apartment and live on Śliska 7, flat 10. We have a large sunny apartment. My mother-in-law is here and Stach with Wisia.

Heniek is with Wandzia and us. There was a plan to live at their place but because even they had to move—they left their apartment to the woman lodger—they are now with us. Not so long ago I had news from Hania. She had a letter from Stefek, I think from Toulouse. He is in good health, is working and is looking for possibilities to communicate with you. We are so happy that there is news from you. How did you get through the hot months? Do you really have work and are able to manage? I suppose that you have become familiar with the language and this makes things easier. From Sewek, I haven't had a letter for a long time, even though from time to time help arrives from there and so I know that they are still there. As for us, we all work a bit and are managing. Probably all sorts of rumours are spread around about us, but it isn't as bad as one might think. We are all in good health, in a positive frame of mind. We are well provided for, and I imagine it will go on like that. Jasia is studying—Maryla is teaching her and three other girls. Apart from that she has a drawing class. Mother is giving a few lessons and takes excellent care of the housekeeping. You asked in the last letter what Mr Bechs[tein] is doing.

He lives in a house of a friend of Sewek's. Because we only occupy one room, part of the furniture has been stored. The street on which we live is considered to be an aristocratic district ... [1] we have masses of acquaintances here, all my colleagues, students, and aunts ... Social contacts blossom, one lives as if in a village. I think, however, that in a little more time we shall start living in a big town again and then we will at last see our nearest and dearest.

Meanwhile, I kiss you warmly—Maryla.

If you are going to write, address it to Hel[ena] Dąbrowska, Piusa XI 25/16 for me. I am not sure whether all the letters sent to me reach my address.

Dear Franeczko! A big kiss for your letter, it gave us a lot of pleasure, I would so like to embrace you!—Heniek

and I too, Ludka and Wandzia

My Darling Franuś! I received today your letter of 12th October written to Ludka. It made me very happy, because it is in your own handwriting. I wrote to you, darling, a few days ago and I don't remember if I included the address Śliska 7. Try to write to this address, perhaps it will get through. Stefek's family lives in the same place as before [i.e., Zofiówka in Otwock]. They are all well. Stefan [Miller] comes often to Warsaw, and Irenka too from time to time, their mother is in the country all the time. Anka

---

1 This is the 'small ghetto', linked with the 'large ghetto' by a pedestrian bridge over ulica Chłodna.

exchanged her room for one of the same sort in our district. We see her often. As of recently, she is working a bit. We are in good health, and that in these times is the most important thing . . . the rest is also somehow not too bad, we are managing. And you darling, how are you managing, it is difficult to imagine.

I kiss and hug you lots and lots —your Ł.W.

for Stefan also hugs from afar.

Letter from Maryla to Franciszka:

4 December 1940

Dear Franeczko, thank you for your last letter; the first calm one, like those of long ago. How wonderful that at last you know about Stefek, and you are not completely alone because you have friends around you. I would like to know whether you have received several letters from us, sent through this route. Please write and tell us about your work, are you drawing?

As Ludka doesn't know where Bolek is, she went to a clairvoyant. That was in September; the woman described the places where you and Stefan are and foretold that you would be in touch in five months. Marysia asked the same woman about Paweł, who is very far away . . . she described in minute detail the place where he is staying, the professions of Sewek, Michał, and Paweł, who it appears is in Russia. We are all in good health and in good spirits. Mother takes care of the housekeeping. Jasia has a lot of friends which makes Maryla very happy . . . one can't have too much of a good thing . . . The apartment we have is large and sunny. We occupy the middle room, next to Heniek's. I like them very much and we are happy together. Jasia's walks are very confined. We wander down the street where we live and the nearest parallel one as they are the best and the most spacious. Łucja and Maryla live on Śliska 7, m.10, write to that address. In every building there is a house committee, a local . . . caretaker and a policeman. We have eight doctors as neighbours, and as far as sanitary conditions are concerned, the house is maintained in exemplary fashion. Soon, the committee will buy goats, so that there won't be a shortage of milk for the children. In Heniek's warehouse I am keeping a pregnant rabbit—for Jasia's sake. This animal gives birth to eight or ten rabbits every six weeks. We don't and won't lack anything. We have a supply of all sorts of important things, humour and patience. In a word, don't worry about us at all. One thing is certain, that in the next generation there will be a shortage of architects, because all children, even babies will have an aversion to building blocks, bricks and partitions . . .

So far, I maintain that providence is looking after us, money always appears before our previous funds are exhausted. Of all that I possessed—I didn't lose anything and didn't sell anything. As for making up for the loss of Father's pictures, a whole life under the protection of providence would not suffice. Jasia is doing schoolwork and drawing. Apart from that, your sister teaches a group of children to draw, one draws from nature (that's how the cookie crumbles—I am thinking of myself). Janka draws very well, it is a real satisfaction—how she knows where, for every movement, to draw arms and legs. Our rabbit lived in the house for a few days, and during biology and drawing lessons, she was drawn from every angle. Now there are few other pleasures. One becomes enthusiastic about lighting the stove—it is not a rare event thanks to Heniek, and our lunch of several courses is always welcomed with a ceremonial speech.

Nevertheless, we are well and content. Please write often. Every day, Mother looks in the mailbox. I kiss you a lot. Maryla

My darlingest Franuś. Thank you so much for your last letter. The first sunny and happy one, now that you know where Stefek is. It is a happy coincidence that he lives with a friend. I should also like to receive a few words from him. We can all now be cheerful, since we have news of our nearest and dearest. Darling, I would also like to know what sort of work you have and how you live. I am thinking about you all the time. When I get a letter I try to imagine how each of you looks, what you wear, because generally everyone has changed and looks different, those who were stout have become slim. Also, when they meet, even as strangers, they communicate with great ease. Not so long ago we also sent a letter to you.

Kisses and embraces from your very loving, Ł.W.

The wall outside our balcony is the partition that divides us from the world. It is on ulica Sienna. After a while I stop noticing it. The street below the balcony is very quiet, unlike the other side of our building which is full of people moving around like ants. Our one-room home is our nest. I am somewhat frightened of the outside world, and at the same time confinement in our room is a problem. Nothing to be done. I get ill. At night my mother moves her bed next to mine, the table is pushed against the wall. Now the passageway to Heniek's room is constricted. I don't know what's wrong with me, nor does anyone else. Cupping[2] my back does little to help. Aspirin achieves nothing. I make a white goat out of cotton-wool with matches for legs, and it walks in and out of a grey box with green paper grass. After a few days, doctors from the building are brought in to see me. One of them brings me three cream cakes. This turns out to be a miracle cure. I get better.

Convalescence consists of roller-skating up and down the tiny hall and performing somersaults on the bed. I sit on the high box bed and eat rice with cinnamon and sugar which my grandmother brings to me. I am getting bored with Africa and just wait for something to happen to break the monotony.

It does. Two members of the Gestapo burst into our flat to conduct a search for fur. Łucja, Maryla, and I are sitting at the table. They tear Maryla's sheepskin waistcoat from her back, stampede around, slam doors and go. I sit paralysed in my chair. Maryla's face is white. Nobody says a word, neither then nor later. The event will never be mentioned, and this sort of silent response to such events becomes our modus vivendi.

---

2   The application of heated suction cups to the body.

Card from Łucja sent to Martinho Severo (F. Themerson), R. dos Lusiadas 78, 1º, Lisbon, Portugal, from Maria Tywonek, Marschallstr. 94, w.31, Warschau, via Berlin:

17 December 1940

> Dear, darling Franko! Warmest thanks for the card which I received a few days ago, also with the news about my most loved ones. I am so happy that they are together and are working. Here everything is all right. Maryla, Jasia and Łucja live on Śliska 7, are in good health and are managing very well. I would very much like to know whether Stefek is where you both were until recently. How is your health? Every bit of news about you makes me happy. Irenka with mother and husband are where they were. They work, and Anka also works a bit and lives with Ginia. Sewek has not changed his address, and Ludka and family live with us. A week ago Maryla sent you a long letter.

> Kisses and hugs from Ł.W.

Letter from Teresa Żarnower in Lisbon to Stefan Themerson in Voiron (this letter includes a copy of letters to Franciszka from Maryla and Łucja):

28 December 1940

> Dear Stefan!
> I received both your letters, one today, one yesterday. The first letter I got last week, I passed to Franka. We talked about you. If you are in good health and have a strong liver

then you can eat bananas, but they are very, very hard to digest. You should consult liver experts.

With me there is nothing new. My life, the entire contents of my life, can be defined in one phrase: I am waiting. What for? FOR A VISA! Damn it! It is true that I am not very hopeful, but I want to go to the other hemisphere. It's not so easy from here. Life is not particularly interesting; the climate agrees with me, although recently even here it has been cold.

I haven't had a letter from Franka for a long time. However, I received a letter from the family. Since I shall be sending this letter to her today, I am copying it word for word for you. [This is the letter from Maryla Chaykin and Łucja Weinles of 24 November 1940.]

At last I finished, wow! It's tiring this copying, but I'm sure it will give you pleasure. I don't have anything to add, so I send you a warm handshake and wish you a happy New Year.

Did you get some sweets and a little tea, and Halina—did she get coffee? Why is this Halina so stingy with the 'written word'? Where is Blanka [Blanche Bronstein] and her family? Do you know by chance where the family of Halina's uncle has ended up? I wrote several times already, but she doesn't answer. Please write about yourself in greater detail and more often. Are you in contact with Franka? If you write please send her my greetings.

Three days later, on 31 December 1940, Teresa Żarnower writes to Franka.

Dear Franka

Yesterday, I received a letter from your family so I am sending it to you. I made a copy for Stefan and will send it to him. Immediately on receiving an answer, I will send it to your mother. From Złotowskis who left nearly seven weeks ago in good material circumstances and with a wealthy man friend I got some dollars, which I shall use to send parcels to your family. There they sell tea for the price of gold. Unfortunately, to my own people I can't send anything because I've had no news from them for the past five months and don't even know where they live now.

With me there is nothing new. Your note that I can't count on American visa via London made me very depressed. Vegetating and constantly waiting.

Yesterday I received a letter from Stefan asking to let you know that he received the money. He would like to eat bananas in the company of black women [i.e., travel to Brazil] and asks for advice. It is difficult to advise in these circumstances. You will talk soon with Mr Freyd. I sent him half a kilo of chocolate. Have you changed your flat. I am surprised that Stefanja Z[ahorska] doesn't answer my letters. I suppose she didn't get them.

I wish you, and all decent people, a happy New Year.

If you could send me a teach-yourself-English book and an Anglo-Polish dictionary, I would be inexpressibly grateful.

Card from Łucja to Franciszka, sent to Martinho Severo (F. Themerson), R. dos Lusiadas 78, 1°, Lisbon, Portugal, via Berlin, from Maria Tywonek, Marschallstr. 94, w.31, Warschau:

22 January 1941, postmarked 3 February 1941

My darling Franka, I wrote to you already several times to this address, I don't know whether you received my letters. I am happy that you already have news from Stefek. We also received Stefek's letter from Hania [Kawa], in which he writes that he feels well and is in communication with his wife. Darling, how are you, are you still working? Most heartfelt thanks for the parcel. I sent part of it to Irenka, I am sure that they were very pleased, especially Mother. Write a few more words about yourself. We feel well, and don't lack anything. We are in contact with Sewek all the time and we live together with Mrs Chajkin, with Stach and Wisia, also with Heniek, Ludka and Wandzia. Each family occupies one room and we have a common kitchen. Jasia is studying in Maryla's class, also drawing with two other girls. What is most important is that we are well, and when we receive frequent news from our loved ones we are happy. Kisses and embraces from Ł.W.

Dear Franeczko, thank you very much for the tea. Don't worry about us. We miss you very much. Kisses, Maryla

---

Maryla suggests that I should write more often to Franciszka. I don't like writing letters and have nothing to say. Reading is my greatest pleasure. We borrow books from a library. I read Henryk Sienkiewicz's *In Desert and Wilderness* and am moved by this travel adventure of two children, a boy and a girl, Staś and Nel. They are brave and resourceful, and when Nel cries and Staś asks her why, she replies that she is not crying, it is only that her eyes are sweating. I try to follow their journey in the atlas which lies open on the box-bed between the two windows of our room.

Card from Łucja to Franciszka, addressed to to Martinho Severo (F. Themerson), R. dos Lusiadas 78, 1°, Lisbon, Portugal, from Maria Tywonek, Marschallstr. 94, w.31, Warschau:

29 January 1941

My dearest Franuś! Last week I sent a card to you, darling. I suppose that you received it. I sent it after receiving a parcel with tea. In the last few days another parcel arrived with cocoa. I am worried that you are depriving yourself; you certainly can't have too much for your own use. Darling, I would like to get another handwritten letter from you. We were delighted to receive Stefek's letter, which Hania sent us, but we don't have his address. I sent some of the tea to Irenka, you can imagine how delighted she was with such a greeting. Here, all is well. We are all healthy, and don't lack anything. We have frequent news from Sewek and he tries to help us materially. Don't worry about us. I would also like to have some more personal news from you and Stefek. I miss you very much, and pray that we might see each other soon, kiss and embrace. Kisses from me, Maryla and Jasia. Your loving, Ł.W.

Best wishes from Teresa Ż[arnower]

Letter to Stefan via Hania Kawa
from Irka, Stefan's mother, Stefan Miller, dated 6 February 1941
from Łucja, dated 14 February 1941
from Maryla to Hania, dated 14 February 1941:

Dear, darling Stefulku, we received today your letter of 16th December. We are so happy that you are well and that somehow you are managing. From Franka we have good news. We are working as before, don't worry about us, we are in good health and are calm. Anka is also well and is working. We communicate by telephone and letter. Huge hugs and Kisses, Irk[a]

My darling dear Stefulku, I kiss you lots and lots of times and ask for news as often as possible. Missing you, Matuś [Stefan's mother]

Dear Stefek! You gave us all a lot of pleasure with your letter. Write as often as possible. I kiss you, Stef[an Miller]

Dearest Hania, I am very worried about you and yours. Thank you for news and please send some more about yourself. Lots of kisses . . . ? Łucja and Irka

Kotulku, darling! lots of kisses and I dream of being able to do it in person, Anka

Dear Stefek, we were all very anxious without news from you. In the end came your little letter, it made me very happy and calmed me and I will be happy when you will be together and may it be soon. Such a long separation is very hard. Darling, write again a few more words, ~~it's so pleasant~~ to receive something handwritten from one's nearest and dearest. I hug and kiss you many times, Ł.W.

Dear Hania, I am sending you warmest best wishes and thanks for news, Ł.W.

Dear Hania

Please forgive me for not giving a sign of life for so long. There are difficulties with sending letters. We managed to change the apartment for a different one with three rooms. Łucja, Maryla and Jasia live on Śliska 7, m. 10. One room I gave to my mother-in-law and brother-in-law, the other to Heniek and Wandzia. We are managing. Jasia is doing schoolwork in a class led by Maryla. Łucja also has some work, and apart from that Sewek remembers us . . . If it wasn't for the fact that we miss Sewek, Franka, and Stefek so much—it would be tolerable. From Franka we have frequent news via Lisbon.

We were very happy to get Stefanek's news. At last one could see his own handwriting. Please, dear Hania, be so very kind and send him the news that we are in good health, that we remember him all the time and ask for frequent news. Stefanek's whole family is in good health. Irka and Stefan are working. Please, dear Hania, send us a few words about you. How is your health, what are you doing, and do you have news from Franka. Kindest regards from me, Mother and Jasia. Maryla

Card from Łucja to Franciszka, addressed to Martinho Severo (F. Themerson), R. dos Lusiadas 78, 1º, Lisbon, Portugal, from Maria Tywonek, Marschallstr. 94, w.31, Warschau:

14 February 1941

My dearest Franeczko! During the last weeks we sent you, my dearest, several letters and I am writing again today because I already received the fourth parcel. We thank you warmly for it, but darling this is really too much. The first parcel I divided up, as I already wrote to you, but this one will be for my own personal use, i.e., I shall exchange it for other things that I need. At the moment, we don't lack anything—both of us, Maryla and I, earn a bit. Jasia is doing schoolwork in Maryla's class. Sewek also keeps us in mind and sends parcels as well. We received two letters from Stefek. You can imagine our delight and happiness. He feels well and apparently has frequent news from his wife. I am so glad that you received our letter, because the last parcel arrived to the address, Śliska 7.

I kiss you, your Ł.W.

I am learning to draw. I am learning French with Mme Jacob who comes twice a week. I am doing schoolwork with another girl, later with three others, and follow a school curriculum preparing for the 4th class. We sit around the table in the centre of the room with Maryla at one end. When I am drawing I copy my mother's style of children's illustration—scenes of folk dancing, children at play, dogs walking in the park. When my mother puts a potato on the table for us to draw, things don't go so well. Dull, black potato—I fill in a black circle, that's it. I am too literal. Maryla explains that the potato is neither black nor grey but blue, two shades of blue as a matter of fact; it is both shiny and dull, that its texture is varied. The result is not satisfactory; I cannot reproduce this sort of subtlety. I prefer to make attractive line drawings of imaginary things than to depict the real world, however small, harmless and domestic.

Card from Łucja to Teresa Żarnower, addressed to Mme Martinho Severo (F. Themerson), R. dos Lusiadas 78, 1º, Lisbon, Portugal, from Maria Tywonek, Marschallstr. 94, w.31, Warschau:

25 February 1941

Dear Madame,

Today I received a card from you and I am replying at once. Thank you so much for news about Franka and Stefek. Please send them greetings and thanks for thinking of us. We are all in good health and greet every bit of news with great joy. Thank you so much for the parcels. Maria Ch. received 3, Łucja W. 3, and yesterday Maria and Ludwika H[aller] again 2, altogether 8. Everything is excellent and we make good use of it. Tea and coffee can be exchanged for other things, but cocoa I am leaving for Jasia. Kindest greetings and embraces for you, Franka and Stefan. Ł.

Best wishes from Maryla and Jasia.

The parcels become an important subject of the correspondence because their arrivals are, apart from letters, the most important events of our lives. The parcels are constantly counted and discussed. Łucja writes about them to Franciszka to reassure her about their arrival, to stress their enormous usefulness. Also, to begin with, to hint and then to describe more fully some of the tensions and difficulties of living with members of this extended family at close quarters.

TRADING WITH THE ENEMY BRANCH
(Treasury and Board of Trade).

Telephone No.:
HOLBORN 4300.

Telegraphic Address:
" TRADENEMY, LONDON."

In any reply (which should be addressed to "THE CON-TROLLER" at the address opposite) please add the letters H.K. to the address on the envelope placing them in the left-hand bottom corner.

The following reference should be quoted in any further communications:—T/E

24, KINGSWAY,
LONDON, W.C.2.

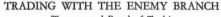
PLE[A]   [Q]UOTE
IN YO[UR] REPLY

5th March 1941.

Gen.21/921/1164

Madam,

The information furnished by you at your interview here on the 3rd March has now been carefully considered.

By the Trading with the Enemy Act, 1939, it is forbidden (without special permission which is not granted save in exceptional cir-cumstances) to have any commercial, financial or other intercourse or dealings with or for the benefit of any person in enemy or enemy occupied territory and it is clear that, in asking friends in United States to send money to Lisbon to be expended in the despatch of parcels of food to your mother in Warsaw, you have infringed these provisions.

It is noted that you claim that you were unaware that arrangements of this kind were
/prohibited

Mrs. Fr. Themerson,
1, Redcliffe,
262, Brompton Road,
S.W.5.

60

```
prohibited but it is, nevertheless, also to
be observed that your friend, Miss U.Lubelska,
with whom you have been living for some
months, had already had some correspondence
with this Branch on a similar subject, when
these very provisions were explained to her,
and, further, that you were aware that she
had had correspondence with this Branch.

        Having regard to all the circumstances,
it is not proposed that any further action
should be taken in this instance and it is
not, therefore, necessary to consider further
the real extent of your knowledge of the pro-
visions of the Act, but it must be clearly
understood that any further activities of
this nature on your part will be regarded
most seriously.

        I am to ask you to be good enough to
acknowledge receipt of this letter.

                I am, Madam,
                   Your obedient Servant,
```

Letter from the Treasury and Board of Trade, Trading with the Enemy Branch, 24 Kingsway, London WC2, to Mrs. Fr. Themerson, 1 Redcliffe, 262 Brompton Road, London SW5, forbidding Franciszka to send parcels to Poland, i.e. enemy territory.

Despite this clear warning and Franciszka's request to Teresa Żarnower to comply with it, parcels continue to be sent and, for the time being, to arrive.

Letter from Maryla and Łucja to Franka, addressed to Martinho Severo (F. Themerson), R. dos Lusiadas 78, 1°, Lisbon, Portugal, from Maria Tywonek, Marschallstr. 94, w.31, Warschau:

5 March 1941

Dear Franeczko, thank you for your last letter of 8th January. We are happy that the letters from you and Stefek arrive. We are well and don't lack anything. Together with Łucja we received seven parcels. Thank you so much. Yesterday, Ludka received a parcel. We are worried all the time that you deprive yourself in order to help us. We are so glad that you have work. I was sure that you would fall on your feet wherever you were. But in the end you had to travel with a rucksack, and it could not have been simple to acquire everything anew. I expect you are learning the language and you can probably communicate without difficulty. Stefek's family lives where they were before, and they work. Anka—Pańska 48, m.66—also works and things are going reasonably well for her. From Sewek we have news constantly, and help. You know very well what letters from our loved ones mean to us now, and it is a real joy that even though you have all gone in different directions—news does arrive. Apart from cards, I sent several long letters, you probably received them.

For the time being we haven't got a photograph to send you. I also doubt that it would arrive. We look well, and Jasia is taller, probably by as much as a head. We live as if in the provinces, we have a lot of acquaintances around and one leads the life of a large family. Please write again.

I kiss you a lot, Maryla

My darling! Your last letter made me very happy, because you wrote it yourself and we learned about certain things. And we too would like to know how you look now, but too bad, one must have patience. My darling, thank you so much for the parcels, everything is excellent, but a bit too much. I worry that you are spending too much and will not have enough for yourself. I am reading your letter many times and every one of your words calms and delights me. Your letter was written two months ago, yet it seems to me as if it was from the last few days. From Stefek we also had a few words, and all this means a great deal now.

I write often, as is my habit, so that you will not worry about us.

I embrace and kiss you a thousand times. Ł

I also wrote to Stefek

My very warm greetings. I have nothing to write about. My song has bored me enough. I grasp your paw, Teresa

How did you resolve the sending of the parcels?!!!

Copy of Franciszka's letter to Teresa Żarnower:

8 March 1941

Dear Teresko, you received my telegram, didn't you? It worked out, as you could gather from my telegram, that it was not even permitted for me to know about parcels for my mother, even though I didn't provide money for them. And so don't send any more, darling. The same applies to letters. I am only allowed to receive them through Cook or the Red Cross.

Apart from that, with me there is nothing new. I continue to work in the ministry. The work is a bit like torture. I've developed a total aversion to compasses and I dream of a decent paintbrush and decent paints.

And what about you! How are you? At last they sent Stefan an affidavit.

I should so much like to receive from you [and Stefan] a joint letter from Lisbon.

Drawing by Franciszka Themerson,
London, 1941

Write something about yourself, my dear, how you are and what you are doing.

A warm embrace—Franka

Nevertheless, parcels via Lisbon continue to arrive in Warsaw until June 1942. By the autumn of 1941, the parcels become the family's sole support. The correspondence provides no further information about the prohibition on letters or packages, but contact with Lisbon remains open nonetheless through the Polish Ministry of Information and Documentation. There is another vital reason for Franciszka to maintain these Portuguese contacts, which is the acquisition of affidavits and visas for Stefan to leave Vichy France and to reach London in the summer of 1942.

Card from Maryla to Franciszka, addressed to Martinho Severo (F. Themerson), R. dos Lusiadas 78, 1º, Lisbon, Portugal, from Maria Chaykin, Śliska 7, w.10, Warschau:

25 March 1941

> Dear Franeczko. Thank you very much for the parcels we have received again, with powdered milk and tea. Everything is all right here, we are healthy, and calm about the coming months—we don't lack anything. This year is much easier than the last one. Sewek is helping us constantly, he is working in his profession. Mother decided to get something for herself, thanks to the parcels you sent. Here it is still very cold but where you are it's probably hot . . . We dwell on that all the time. We also heard recently from Stefek. We really need these letters now for our well being. I sent recently two long letters to you, but I don't know if they arrived. Darling, don't send us parcels all the time, you will run out of money, and we have much more than before. I kiss you a lot, Maryla

> Kisses and hugs for my darling Franeczka. Ł.W.

Card from Łucja to Franciszka, addressed to Martinho Severo (F. Themerson), R. dos Lusiadas 78, 1°, Lisbon, Portugal, from Maria Tywonek, Marschallstr. 94, w.31, Warschau:

27 March 1941, postmarked 11 April 1941
My darling Franeczko!

Yesterday we sent a card to you, but as there is an opportunity I am writing a few words. I received your letter from 1 January and during that time 9 parcels. Darling, all the time it seems to me that by doing all this, you deprive yourself of the most essential things.

Thank you very much darling for everything, but don't worry about us. Just imagine, with one parcel I was able to buy myself a new pair of glasses, to be able to read in the evening. The old ones were no longer suitable. I went to an oculist in our building. Now I intend to exchange another parcel for shoes. I would very much like to receive another long letter from you, but one has to wait so long. From Stefanek, as I wrote to you, there was his handwritten letter. It gave me enormous pleasure. His mother is together with Irenka and her husband, where they have been till now, and Anka lives here and works. I gave her greetings from you in the form of tea.

Hugs and kisses from Ł.W.

I take our situation for granted. I pretend not to notice the anxiety that surrounds our life. It is the norm. Back to Australia and the atlases on the box bed, to the garden, the incipient garden on the balcony. I do schoolwork, make puppets, and read. I am busy, I am at home with Maryla, and everything is fine.

I don't remember the names of my friends and have a feeling that there weren't as many as Maryla thinks. But one fine spring day several of us got together with the caretaker's family to make paper flowers. From somewhere he managed to get some coloured paper, wire, and tissue. The project was completed in one afternoon. There were several bouquets of bright, colourful flowers. My flowers were yellow with black centres. They were not ours to keep, and at the end of the afternoon, the remnants of paper were cleared away, the flowers were collected by the gatekeeper's wife, and having been thanked for our brave efforts, we dispersed.

Card from Łucja to Franka, addressed to Martinho Severo (F. Themerson), R. dos Lusiadas 78, 1°, Lisbon, Portugal, from Maria Tywonek, Marschallstr. 94/31, Warschau:

18 April 1941, postmarked 13 May 1941

> My dearest Franuś! I take advantage of every opportunity to write a few words to you. I write very often but don't know if my cards and letters reach you. From you, darling, I had recently one letter written on the 1st of January and one has to wait so long for the next one . . . Don't worry about us. This winter perhaps was lighter for us than the last one and I hope that we shall continue to manage, perhaps even our separation won't last so long. How are you my dear, how do you live, do you have frequent news from

Stefek? From Sewek we have letters and cards quite often, he also helps us from time to time. Recently you've been sending so many parcels (I think there were 12), so that already I have managed to do the most important things such as remaking of some clothes, shoes, etc. Thank you so much for everything, but I can imagine how this causes you to cut down your own spending, so don't do it anymore. Irenka with mother and husband are where they have been so far.

Lots of kisses and hugs. Ł.W.

Franko! Ask the bearer of this letter, the very honourable Mr E.F. [Ernest Freyd] if the matter of the funds has been resolved. I sent the little book to Stefan already. Teresa.

Card from Maryla to Franciszka, addressed to Martinho Severo (F. Themerson), R. dos Lusiadas 78, 1°, Lisbon, Portugal, from Maria Chaykin, Śliska 7, w.10, Warschau:

12 May, postmarked 17 May 1941, received by Lisbon post office 19 July 1941

Dear Franeczko. It's already a long time since we had a letter from you, even though parcels are coming all the time and they are also greetings from you. All of us are in good health. Since changing apartments we are doing well thanks to the fact that Sewek and Michał are working and sending help. Your parcels are a great help for Mother. As far as you are able, please write how is your health and your work. A few weeks ago we had a letter from Stefek in his own hand.

He writes that all is well with him, that he is in good health and that everything is all right with you. I kiss you a lot, Maryla

Hugs and lots of kisses for my darling from Ł.W.

Card from Łucja to Franka, addressed to Martinho Severo (F. Themerson), R. dos Lusiadas 78, 1º, Lisbon, Portugal, from Maria Tywonek, Marschallstr. 94/31, Warschau:

postmarked 28 May 1941

My dearest Franuś! I had in the last few days a letter from Stefek, which made me extraordinarily happy. My darling, how are you, do you still live in the same place? I replied to Stefek immediately. His family is well, we too. We often write to Sewek and receive help from him. Thank you very much for the parcels, which arrive so often. I received the last one on the 23rd of April. My darling, write a few words and don't send us so much, because you won't be able to look after yourself.

Thousands of kisses and hugs from Ł.W.

Card from Łucja to Franka, addressed to Martinho Severo (F. Themerson), R. dos Lusiadas 78, 1º, Lisbon, Portugal:

25 May, received by Lisbon post office 28 June 1941

My dearest Franeczko! Your handwritten letter from 24th April, made me so happy that I couldn't do anything for the whole day. So many parcels this month, darling. How can you spend so much money on this, and not only for us, you even sent Ludka, I think, 4 parcels, that is impossible from the earnings of one person! I had a letter from Stefek. I wrote back immediately, but the card was returned. After a few days there was news from H[ania] that he left. I am so glad that you have frequent news from your husband. How are you, now with that work of yours, do you do housekeeping [together] at home? Because here we have 3 households, each one for themselves in their own way. I gave your letter to Stefan [Miller], because he just happened to be here, and Maryla took it to Anka and persuaded her to write back immediately. Anka is working. Ginia lives and works here at Stefan's in the office. Władek works in the hospital office. Jasia is in good health, is doing lessons and drawing. I kiss you and hug you very much. We often call her Franka by mistake! Ł.W.

Kisses from Jasia

Letter from Maryla to Franciszka, addressed to Martinho Severo (F. Themerson), R. dos Lusiadas 78, 1°, Lisbon, Portugal, from Maria Chaykin, Śliska 7, w.10, Warschau:

3 June 1941

Dear Franeczko, thank you very much for your letter of 24th April, which we received last week. We wrote back at once, but my card, presumably not sufficiently objective, was returned. I haven't received your letter sent on 16th April. Last week, Mother in her card confirmed receipt of all recent parcels, but since then more coffee and cocoa arrived. If only we could be sure that we are not taking the butter from your bread. I had already written, my dear, that Łucja and Maria are all the time in contact with Sewek and that they don't lack for anything. Only a week ago spring arrived, and it has been harder than ever to wait for it this time. We have a small sunny balcony, which as far as possible Jasia uses as an outlet for her energies. Several times a day she plants the same beans and waters them the appropriate number of times. She works as if in a real garden but if anything will actually grow—I very much doubt it. Apart from that, she plays in the courtyard between a lilac bush and a chestnut tree. There are some gardens, but I am worried about large gatherings of children and whooping cough. We shall probably keep to our vegetable garden on the balcony. Till now I haven't done any drawing at all, only as much as was necessary for chats on natural history or for games with multiplication tables. We played around a bit with Plasticine. Jasia and her friends made country villages and other landscapes in four colours on serving plates. Soon, Jasia will have a vacation and so I will be free too.

Mother is doing housekeeping, so I shall be drawing a bit; it is always pleasant, irrespective of how good one is at it. Jasia has a lot of friends, they have all learned to draw. They go for walks with an exercise book and crayons and they all want to become painters. And what am I doing creating competition for my own daughter? Soon I shall have our photograph for you, I will send it at the first opportunity. It will convince you that we don't look worse

71

than always, a few white hairs more or less don't count. Only Janka and the palm have grown—they are the same height. I got a skirt and blouses for Jasia, and you can probably imagine how grownup she is. As for me, I got some pink linen and I am making myself a dress, I am also getting a white blouse to go with a costume. With Mother it's more difficult, but she agreed to have a blouse made from my black and white silk summer dress, which perhaps you remember. As far as new things go, we still managed to get some very nice, dark covers for the windows. They are very pretty and fashionable . . . You know, of course, that we have a very sunny apartment.

As far as our loved ones are concerned, all in Otw[ock] are in good health and at their posts, they work and kill time, which recently has been moving a bit slowly. Anka works in the local administration office—opposite the windows of Father's studio. I took your card to her. She is going to write. Ginia lives on Elektoralna 6, she works in Stefan's office. Heniek's family, as before, is living with us, but from time to time we quarrel, or rather they are furious, and we don't know what it's about. This will probably pass, but there is nothing like living separately. I haven't talked to Stach for a year. The only platform for good relations between us is the rendezvous of our mothers in the kitchen, with saucepans and kettles. Frequent cards arrive from Hania, and she has changed her address. I wrote to you my dear, that I learned that Stefanek went to Mrs Marseille. We await news of him with impatience. Olek, our cousin, works hard in a factory at night. Lutek and Cela are already free. They are going toward the south-west, and are waiting for the ice to move [for the end of the debacle?]. Goodness knows when that might be, perhaps in July. Maria, Michał's old friend, is with them, also Lusia's, Olek's wife's, entire family. Also far, but in a better climate is Paweł. Your friend, Lonia N[adelman/Janecka] is with Sewek.

Your friend, Jurek's mother, died nearly a year ago. You asked about it several times. I didn't want to write about it on a card. At the next opportunity I shall again write at length. It is difficult to imagine now that once we lived together, that one knew about every skin rash and sore throat; and now I don't know anything, how you look and if you are in good health. Perhaps you will get this letter just in time for your birthday [28 June]. Best birthday wishes, loving kisses—Maryla

Darling Franeczko, soon I will send you my photograph. Thank you for the wonderful chocolate. Loving kisses—Jasia

I embrace and kiss you, my darling, a thousand times and thank you very much for new parcels. Ł.W.

It is Ludka's birthday and a present has to be found. Maryla suggests that I could give her the small Chinese vase which is standing empty on a shelf of my cupboard. I think about it. I don't really like this small object with blue and gold decorations. I am happy to give it to Ludka. There is no card but the vase is decorated with a bow made of string, and I sing 'Sto lat!' [May you live a hundred years] outside the door of her room.

Letter from Maryla, Łucja, and Jasia to Franciszka, addressed to Martinho Severo (F. Themerson), R. dos Lusiadas 78, 1°, Lisbon, Portugal, from Maria Chaykin, Śliska 7, w.10, Warschau:

18 June 1941

Dear Franeczko, as there is an opportunity, I am writing again. With us everything is all right, we are well and don't lack anything. Between 7 June and today, we received two parcels of tea, three of coffee, and three of chocolate; apart from this Ludka received two, and Anka one. I give you these numbers without comment, because I noticed that comments increase the tempo of despatch [sic]. Thank you so much! With us there is nothing new, perhaps only tomato plants sent by Irka.

Darling, again, only by letter can I wish you all the best for 28 June—for the time being I wish for you only that finally Stefek will find his way to you. Nearly half of the summer has passed, but one doesn't see any decisive changes. We all believe, however, that in a bit longer the most important things will change. Until recently it was cool, we are very happy to have the sun. What's more we don't see much more greenery than in the heads of lettuces, but even this will change. Once more we thank you very much for help.

A big kiss—your Maryla

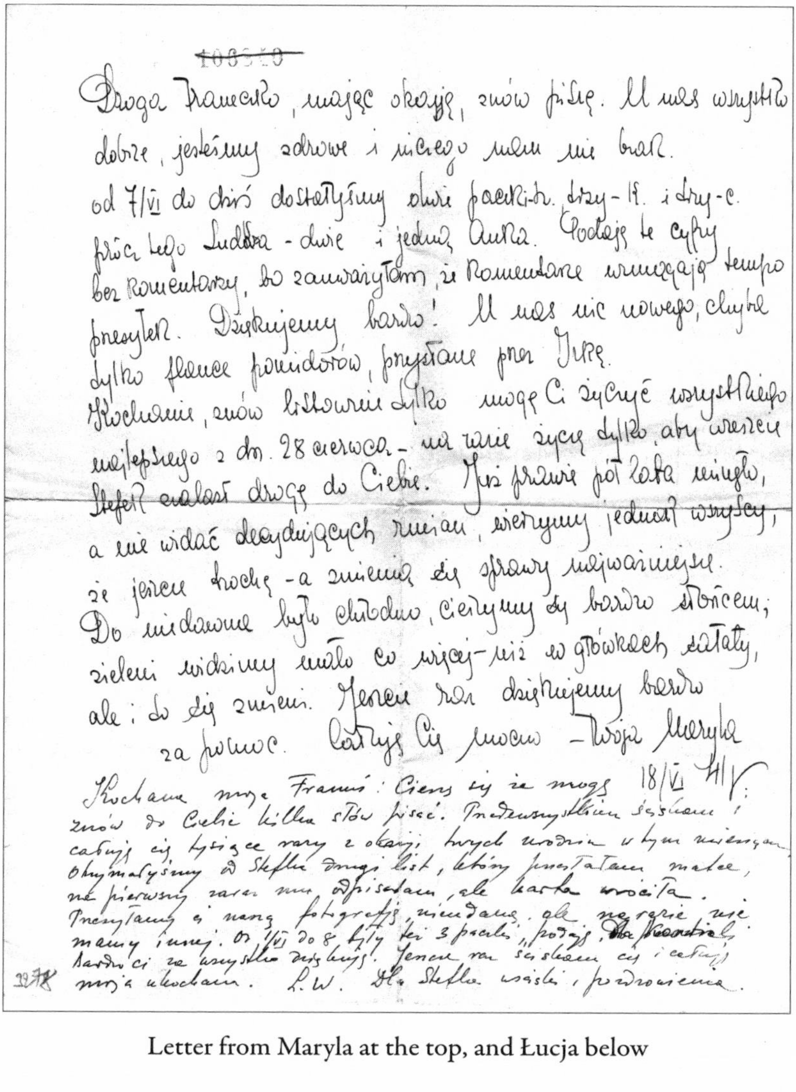

Droga Franeczko, mając okazję, znów piszę. U nas wszystko dobrze, jesteśmy zdrowe i niczego nam nie brak.
Od 7/VI do dziś dostałyśmy dwie paczki-tzn. trzy-ki i trzy-c. Prócz tego Ludka - dwie i jedną Anka. Podaję te cyfry bez komentarzy, bo zauważyłam, że komentarze wstrzymują tempo przesyłek. Dziękujemy bardzo! U nas nic nowego, chyba tylko flance pomidorów, przysłane przez Ikę.
Kochanie, znów listownie tylko mogę Ci życzyć wszystkiego najlepszego z dn. 28 czerwca - na razie życzę tylko, aby wreszcie Stefek znalazł drogę do Ciebie. Już prawie pół roku minęło, a nie widać decydujących zmian, wierzymy jednak wszyscy, że jeszcze trochę - a zmienią się sprawy najważniejsze.
Do niedawna było chłodno, cieszymy się bardzo słońcem; zieleni widzimy mało co więcej - niż w główkach sałaty, ale i to się zmieni. Jeszcze raz dziękujemy bardzo za pomoc. Całuję Cię mocno - Twoja Maryla

Kochana moja Franiu! Cieszę się że mogę 18/VI 41 r. znów do Ciebie kilka słów pisać. Przedewszystkiem ściskam i całuję cię tysiące razy z okazji twych urodzin w tym miesiącu. Otrzymałyśmy od Stefka drugi list, który przesłałam matce, na pierwszy zaraz mu odpisałam, ale karta wróciła. Przesyłamy ci naszą fotografię, nieudaną, ale na razie nie mamy innej. Od 1/VI do 8 były też 3 paczki, podaję, [illegible] bardzo ci za wszystko dziękuję. Jeszcze raz ściskam cię i całuję moja ukochana. Ł.W. Dla Stefka uściski i pozdrowienia.

Letter from Maryla at the top, and Łucja below

Kochana moja Franeczko, tak dawno już Ciebie
nie widziałam, bardzo za Tobą tęsknię.
Tak bardzo chcę Cię zobaczyć, że gdybyś przyjechała,
to bym Ci pozwoliła codziennie ciągnąć się
za warkocze. Dziękuję Ci za świetne kakao,
dostaję je dwa razy dziennie na deser po czubatej
łyżeczce. Czasami Babcia nie wie, że Mamusia
już mi dała i dostaję drugą porcję.
Przeszłam do IV klasy i mam już wakacje.
Mamusia uczy mnie muzyki i języka tego kraju,
w którym byłaś dawniej, oprócz tego rysuję,
pielęgnuję swój śliczny ogródek na balkonie i robię
kukiełki. Mam już jedną kukłę czarownicę
Pomperiposę. Winszuję Ci urodzin, które mają
niedługo nastąpić, tegoż dnia, jeżeli będzie ciepło,
dostanę lody. Całuję Cię mocno   Jasia.

Letter from me, 18 june 1941

My darling Franuś! I am glad to be able to write a few words to you again. First of all I embrace you and kiss you a thousand times for your birthday this month. We received a second letter from Stefek which I forwarded to his mother. I replied at once to his first letter, but the card was returned. We are sending you our photograph that didn't come out very well, but for the time being we don't have another. Between the 1st and 8th June there were also three parcels. I list this just so that you can keep track. Thank you very much for everything. Once more I embrace you and kiss you my darling.

For Stefek hugs and best wishes, Ł.W.

My darling Franeczko. I haven't seen you for such a long time. I miss you very much. I so much want to see you that if you came here I would let you pull my plaits every day. Thank you for the marvellous cocoa. I get a heaped teaspoonful twice a day. Sometimes Granny doesn't know that Mummy already gave it to me and I get a second portion.

I have graduated to 4th class and am now on holiday. Mummy is teaching me music and the language of the country where you were before. Apart from that I draw, look after my lovely garden on the balcony, and make puppets. I already have one puppet, a witch, Pomperimpossa. I wish you all the best for your birthday which is coming soon. On that day, if it is warm I will get ice cream.
Lots of kisses, Jasia

Łucja, Maryla, Jasia, 1941

The photograph which eventually reaches Franciszka has a dual purpose. Apart from reassuring her that we are all right, Franciszka tells me later that it could possibly have been used to produce three travel documents, should such an opportunity have arisen.

Meanwhile, I begin not to behave very well. Doing schoolwork and sitting on the box bed with atlases is getting to bore me. I start running between our room and the bathroom where I wash my hands, there and back, there and back. After some fifteen ablutions, which I count with great care, I stop. Now I shall draw my hands spread out on the table.

Card from Anka to Franciszka, addressed to Martinho Severo (F. Themerson), R. dos Lusiadas 78, 1º, Lisbon, Portugal from A. Poznańska, Pańska 48/6b:

22 June 1941, postmarked 22 July 1941

Franeczko, darling Franeczko!

Although I never for one moment stop thinking about you, today especially I am wholeheartedly with you both. [The 22nd of June is the Themersons' wedding anniversary.] I am drinking aromatic tea and I smell the coffee, but there is no one to make it for, and I weep from missing you.

Darling girl—you must write to me. How are you managing? You have so many responsibilities of your own, and now you send things to me too. Thank you, from the bottom of my heart, thank you—but that is not enough. Think more about yourself, you are probably very thin already.

Lots of kisses, Kotulkowa[3] Anka

Card from Łucja to Franciszka, addressed to Martinho Severo (F. Themerson), R. dos Lusiadas 78, 1º, Lisbon, Portugal, from Weinles Leonia, Śliska 7, m.10, Warschau:

20 July 1941

My darling Franuś. Yesterday, we received your letter of 18th June, the one before, to the family and to us, was dated 22nd April. I was waiting all last week for news from you. We wrote many times in June, several cards and 2 letters.

---

3 The feminine form of 'Kotulek,' Anka's nickname for Stefan.

Even Jasia wrote a big letter and we sent our photograph. My darling, you help us so much with the parcels and so many of them. Ludka received many of them, without even thinking to thank you. Jasia is on holiday now, so Maryla is also free. I go out only twice a week with Beba [a beautiful red-haired girl who was a piano student of Maryla's before the war; her lessons are presumably continuing with Łucja] and apart from that I occupy myself with housekeeping, and I have learned to clean and to cook very well.

I am so happy when I receive a letter from you. If you could be together with Stefek, I would be terribly glad because separation is a terrible thing. How is your health my darling? Are you going away for long? Look after yourself, because when one loses one's strength, it is difficult to regain it. I shall see Anka one of these days. She is working and it is difficult to find her at home. I know that she had a greeting from you already some time ago. And Ginia went to Władek for a holiday. The rest of the family is also well, everyone is in good health. I hug you as much as possible and kiss you many times and send hugs and kisses from me to Stefek. Maryla will write a card separately. On 22nd June I delivered flowers from you. Also on 7th July. Łucja [(22nd June is Franciszka's and Stefan's wedding anniversary; 7th July is the anniversary of the death of Jakub Weinles. The flowers were taken by Łucja to his grave].

Then, Lola, the Dresden china doll, is sold. When the buyer arrives in our room, I stand on my bed and protest passionately, but to no avail. Lola is sold, and Łucja is reduced to having to explain to me why such a step is necessary. I am embarrassed, yes I should have known better, yes I did know better, but I couldn't stop myself. Do I mourn Lola? No, I forget about her quite quickly. There are other things to think about.

'Do you believe in God?' I ask my grandmother the same day, by way of changing the subject. I don't remember her answer, perhaps there was no answer. Something else must have interrupted our conversation because I don't ask again, and God would not be mentioned at all for another few months, when my concern with the subject would become mandatory.

Card from Maryla to Franciszka, addressed to Martinho Severo (F. Themerson), R. dos Lusiadas 78, 1º, Lisbon, Portugal from Maria Chaykin, Śliska 7, w.10, Warschau:

23 July 1941, postmarked 13 August 1941

Dear Franeczko, a few days ago we received a long letter from you. However, we receive greetings several times a week. Letters arrive once every two months—the others don't reach us. And we too send letters to you several times a month. In the last one was a photograph of the three of us. If there will be an opportunity to send a letter, I will send you one more photograph, perhaps at least one will arrive. We are well and in good spirits. Mother is sending a card at the same time as mine. Next month I start work. I suppose that I shall have more of it than before. I lost contact with Sewek a month ago. I suppose that sooner or later I will get news of him from you. From Stefek we received a long letter via Hania K[awa]. A big kiss. Your Maryla

---

Card from Łucja to Franciszka, addressed to Martinho Severo (F. Themerson), R. dos Lusiadas 78, 1º, Lisbon, Portugal, from Ł. Weinles, Śliska 7, Warschau:

9 August 1941, postmarked 27 August 1941

My darling Franeczko! I wrote you a card a week ago, darling. A letter had already arrived from you, also one from Stefek and Hania. I sent letters immediately to St[efan] and Irenka. My child, I wanted to ask you. Why does Ludka receive so many parcels, this week already the fourth, could it not be a mistake? It is impossible after all for you to help so many people, sister, mother. They, the Hs, are together and each one is managing, Wandzia also earns. We give you heartfelt thanks for the help, during those last two months it was very useful. From September, it might be easier for us. Here, we are amazed that you help the family H. so much. You must certainly skimp on what you need most. Darling, please don't economise at your own expense, because afterward it is difficult to catch up. How is Stefek, his letter made us very happy. Pass on kisses and hugs from us. I saw Anka. I believe she wrote to you, and she got the parcels.

We are well. Jasia is on holiday. She spends most of her time on the balcony where she is taking care of little plants, and twice a day goes for a walk down our street. She is healthy and cheerful. I am occupied all day with housekeeping, even though we only have one room, because in the kitchen three families do their domestic chores. It is good that there are no strangers. I kiss you darling, many times. Ł.W.

Next week, Maryla will write a big letter.

Why does Ludka receive so many parcels? Probably because the arrangements for their dispatch from Lisbon are automatic. After the letter from the Board of Trade it is unlikely that Franciszka is personally in control of which parcels go to whom on her original list.

Card from Łucja to Franciszka, addressed to Martinho Severo (F. Themerson), R. dos Lusiadas 78, 1º, Lisbon, Portugal, from Maria Tywonek, Marschallstr. 94/31, Warschau:

19 August 1941

My darling Franeczko, I wrote a card to you recently but I don't know if you received it. I suppose that you have already returned from holiday. I am very interested to know what you did, if you rested and recovered. My darling, write and tell me if you are in good health, because all the time I imagine that you don't look at all well. You worry about everybody else. We look relatively well, even Jasia, despite spending the whole summer in town. We have in our building many acquaintances and Jasia also has many friends who visit her often. From Sewek, news arrived only today. What is happening to Stefek? I sent his letter to his mother. Everybody there is well.

Darling, I don't know if you can imagine how much you have helped us recently. These three months we have maintained ourselves almost totally because of your help. Next month, Maryla will probably already have some work because the holidays are ending. For me it is a bit more difficult. I heard that it is difficult to send what we are receiving. You could divide things into three parts and address some to Jasia. As far as Ludka is concerned, your efforts to send them parcels are unnecessary. They are managing very well anyway. My dear, I kiss you many times and hug you warmly. Convey also hugs and kisses to Stefek. Ł.W.

Letter from Maryla to Franciszka, addressed to Martinho Severo (F. Themerson), R. dos Lusiadas 78, 1°, Lisbon, Portugal, from Maria Chaykin, Śliska 7, w.10, Warschau:

20 August 1941

Dear Franeczko, I hadn't written to you for a long time, and of those letters that I do write—hardly any reach you. Today, I am writing this letter—tomorrow I will see Marysia [Tywonek] . . . We are well and in good shape, once more I am sending you our photograph. It is not too good. All three of us look better and more cheerful in reality. For a long time I haven't had news from Sewek. I didn't have the slightest idea in which part of the world he is. As for Jasia's father [this is a deliberately confusing circumlocution, to suggest that a different person is being mentioned]—today the news came that he is with Michał and his wife in Kraków. Tomorrow, I will get a letter . . . It seems near, but in reality is so very far . . . About Łucja, with her daughter and granddaughter, it is the younger daughter that helps her a great deal. This help is sufficient for practically everything. After a two-month break, I will be starting work in a few days. I expect that I shall have more work than before. Mother is busy and hardworking as always. [It seems] that all her energy was passed on to you, and to me was left nothing more than wonder at that sort of talent. Jasia spends time in a garden, takes care of tomatoes on the balcony and goes to eurythmics classes. I think that next summer she will go to the country, those will be long and well deserved vacations. I believe that Maniek Tr [?], my contemporary and friend from years ago, lives where you are now. Do you meet him? My darling, write and tell us what you are doing. Did you go away for a holiday? Do you have news of Stefanek? We had recently a letter from him, sent to Hania. I see Anka frequently. She works, is in good health, and complains a lot that she can't manage to write to you more often and thank you for the parcels. She is terribly lazy but very nice. The days slip by, one doesn't know how. We read a lot of books and we go out often onto the street, to ask the acquaintances one meets: what's new . . . At the same time as sending the letter to you I am sending a card to your brother-in-law. I am persuading him to spend the rest of the vacation with his brother in the countryside. I should like him to listen to me.

In connection with my wish to have more work than before, I went to the woman director of the New School—on Rysia of yore, the same school where Jasia was in kindergarten. I took Jasia's exercise books. I was told that I was a serious candidate (!) and as soon as the school opens I shall be engaged, something about nature studies and drawing . . . Most pleased of all is Jasia, that we will be going to school together sometimes—what an unbelievable coward! Apart from that nothing new. I should like to be a year older, for time to pass. It's boring, this monotony. Write often, to lighten [our days].

I kiss you a lot—your Maryla

Maryla doesn't get the job teaching at the school, even though it seems to have been promised to her. At least she was led to believe that, being the best candidate, she need not worry about the outcome. She is obviously upset. The subject is not mentioned again.

On the balcony there is only one tomato plant. I am certain that it will bear fruit and when it is big and red, I intend to draw it. In the event, the tomato is not permitted to reach its full, magnificent size because it gets eaten. I wonder if there will be enough time to grow another, but I don't try. The tomato episode is over.

Card from Anka to Franciszka, addressed to Martinho Severo (F. Themerson), R. dos Lusiadas 78, 1°, Lisbon, Portugal, from Anka Poznańska, Pańska 48/6b, Warszawa:

Thursday, 21 August 1941

Dear little Franeczko! Today I received your 16th parcel. I am very, very grateful as I exchange them for tasty soups, vegetables, etc and in that way keep myself going. I wrote to you many times, but I haven't received a single personal letter from you. I am in frequent touch with Luciunia [Łucja] and I read everything that you write to her. Franeczko, brave Franeczko, with pride I tell everyone that not only are you coping yourself but you also help everybody else. If only you could be together with Kotulek as soon as possible—I never stop worrying about it.

Here, we are all in good health. I talk with Irka on the telephone every week and I see Stefan [Miller] from time to time. I had a card from Hania [Kawa]. I thought that she had already visited you but it seems she is comfortable at her sister's.

Write, darling. I kiss you lots and lots. Anka

Letter from Łucja to Franciszka, addressed to Martinho Severo (Fr. Themerson), R. dos Lusiadas 78, 1°, Lisbon, from Ł. Weinles, Śliska 7, w.10, Warschau:

22 August 1941

Darling, darling Franeczko. I have in front of me your last letter of 18 June. Now I am again awaiting news from you. I write very often, several times each month. A few days ago, Maryla sent you a letter and I, a card. I don't know, darling, which of them will arrive, and that is why in some of them I repeat the same things. How did you pass your holidays, I think about it all the time since I received your letter. Did you have a rest, did you recover, because somehow I can't imagine that you really went away. How is everything with Stefek? There was a letter from him via Hania and I sent it on to his mother. Irenka and her husband work in the same place as before. Mother is with them and Władek also has a position there. You write that you would like to know how we live. As you know we live together with family. This is not so simple. Everybody has a room and housekeeping is organised separately. When we changed apartments, Stach took the best room, the most convenient and very large. Anyway, Maryla gave it to him willingly because his mother is with him, who is good and considerate to her. The room in the middle is ours, and the third, beyond ours, is occupied by Ludka with Heniek and Wandzia. It seemed to us that they were well disposed toward us, that we would be happy together. Superficially, our relationship could not be better, but they behave like strangers to us. For their friends they try to do everything they can, but with us they are very calculating. We have a common stove and when during the winter we had no more coal, and there was still a lot in their cellar, the stove was no longer lit. For gas they also pay only a third of what Maryla pays, even though they use more of it because they are in better circumstances than we are. They go in and out through our room from 6 in the morning on, and in the evening when we are going to bed their guests arrive and leave very late without any consideration for us at all. We like Ludka and this is why we pay no attention, especially since we became used to giving way to everyone about everything to preserve peace in the house.

Until recently we had a lot of help from Sew[ek] and Mich[ał]. We didn't lack anything. The last three months however we've lived almost entirely thanks to your help. I wrote to you, my darling, several times that I am surprised that you help Ludka so much. If you want to send so much, send some of it in Jasia's name. Parcels are delivered to the house and Janina would benefit and it would be possible to buy more for her. Friends and acquaintances who are here sometimes by chance when parcels arrive say that it must be a misunderstanding and ask what is it that binds you to Ludka that you help her like your own sister, because she receives just as many, and after all Heniek and Wandzia are working and earning.

I write about this now because until now Maryla didn't let me mention anything about it, because you must know what you are doing. Apart from that, we are in good health. Jasia sits during part of each day on the balcony where she is growing tomatoes. In August Maryla signed her up for gymnastics because she has very little exercise and in September she will start schoolwork in Maryla's class. I do what I can to get some inexpensive coal. I also receive a certain sum from mutual aid every month and a parcel twice a month. Every little bit helps. I have no teaching now, because students are difficult to find. We are managing, and from September perhaps Maryla will have some work. We sent you a photograph. We all look not too bad. I kiss you darling many times and hug you even more. Kisses for Stefek, Your M[other]

I have little to add to the description of our living conditions in Łucja's letter. Maryla does whatever she can to keep relations civil between the families. It is essential for our welfare, and for our survival. But I too will learn in due course that in the face of danger a family can become nothing more than a number of frightened individuals. Meanwhile, I live in another world. I am not aware of these tensions, or, if I am, I try to ignore them. Why are there no parcels addressed to me? Perhaps I am too young to receive them. They have to be collected from somewhere and signed for, I decide. That must be the reason. The real reason is different, of course. Franciszka imagines that we live as a single, close, loving family unit with everyone helping everyone else. She must think that it is better to send the parcels to the same address under different names.

I've no idea what sort of work Heniek and Wandzia do. Ludka rarely leaves the house but Wandzia and Heniek are usually out.

I have no interest in practical things, I imagine a forest of tomatoes growing on the balcony, pine trees below, a wood full of mushrooms and small, friendly Alsatian dogs. My head is a theatre. There are six young boys, the Alsatians, a small drummer at the head with me following, and we march through the streets and out of town. Such scenarios have no conclusion. We never actually arrive anywhere because a new adventure begins.

Card from Łucja to Franciszka, addressed to Mme Martinho Severo (F. Themerson), R. dos Lusiadas 78, 1°, Lisbon, Portugal, from Maria Tywonek, Marschallstr. 94, w.31, Warschau:

27 August 1941

> My darling Franuś, I wrote recently many times, but I want you to receive something at least, so I am sending a card once again. I would like to know if you are back from vacation, how you feel now, and if you feel at least a bit better. Do you now have frequent news from Stefek? How is he, and perhaps you will see each other soon? We will all be very happy then. Write to me about everything, I haven't had a letter from you for a long time. The last letter written by you was from 18th June. I carry it in my handbag and read it all the time. We are well. Recently, Maryla had news from her husband that he is still where he was. The same is the case with Irenka and her husband, they work as before, and Mother lives with them. Anka also works here, and she receives everything you send. Darling, once more I

want to touch on the matter of parcels. At the beginning I was very worried that you economise too much in order to send things to us. Now, recently this help was very useful. We survived during the last months almost entirely because of it. I write about it again because I don't know whether you received the last letter. On the other hand, you send so much to Ludka unnecessarily. They are in much better circumstances than we are. You could send them instead of to her, in Jasia's name to the house, and with identification paper one can collect them. Don't worry if it should be interrupted suddenly, we will manage.

Kisses, kisses, Ł.W.

There is no record of the number of parcels sent on Franciszka's behalf from Lisbon to Warsaw for 1941. However, there are documents indicating that during the first few months of 1942 some 120 parcels are sent, for which Franciszka will still be settling her account with the Polish Ministry of Work and Social Welfare in 1943.

Letter from Maryla to Franciszka, addressed to Martinho Severo (F. Themerson), R. dos Lusiadas 78, 1º, Lisbon, Portugal, from Maria Chaykin, Śliska 7, w.10, Warschau:

1 September 1941

Dear Franeczko, thank you very much for the letter of 28th July, that we received in reply to ours dated end of April. We receive news from you once every two months and it seems that you receive it from us no more often. We are well and everything is all right. It appears that Sewek is still where he was . I received two letters from him in August. He is in good health and in a positive frame of mind. Perhaps we will see each other soon, unfortunately. [Maryla doesn't want him to enter the ghetto.] Everything now is difficult and uncertain. At any rate I no longer have the same peace of mind I had until recently. I sent a letter by a roundabout route and will probably receive a reply quite soon. Anyway, for a little while still, the post will continue to function. I am not giving you the address because it was changed. Anyway, perhaps soon you will be able to write to us all together. We are well and thanks to you we are managing very well. Mother is running the housekeeping extremely well and has problems with Maryla, because she has a taste for vanilla and cinnamon, and here one cannot get it . . . If it would happen that the post would function less well and we wouldn't have help—please don't worry, we will manage. We will be helped by Mr Bechs[stein] or Mr Longin, or other devoted friends who are in more or less better circumstances. Today, I started work with Jasia in the same group as before, and think that with time something will come of it. As far as possible, we are trying to organise normal conditions for Jasia. She is learning to play the piano, drawing, and learning a language. As far as we are concerned, we live for today and, without anticipating the future, we greet with joy every letter from you and Sewek. We borrow books from the library and reminisce about the old days. And to think that it was usually I who was dissatisfied then, and that I was usually right to feel that way. Whereas now I have learned that one must be pleased when one is not worried about one's dearest ones, and if one can even look at them, then what more can one want . . . Today begins the third year of these, so to say, misunderstandings, and yet perhaps they will finish soon. —Don't worry about us darling. We thank you for everything. Many kisses, Maryla

I kiss and give you the warmest hug, and thank you for so many greetings which we receive almost daily. Ł.W.

So now there is a plan to sell the Bechstein grand (Mr Bechst) and Sewek's watch (Mr Longin). Perhaps this is what Sewek is trying to accomplish, since he is still outside. But soon enough he comes to live with us in the ghetto. It is probably October 1941. I paint a notice that is pinned to the door, saying WEL-COME (witaj nam). One of the letters is inverted and I want to redo it but there is no more paper. Now, four of us sleep in our room and I am the only person for whom there is enough space. Sewek sleeps on the box bed, which is disassembled every night. My white cupboard is no longer really mine, it hasn't been mine for some time. It contains our store of food, whatever there is. For my birthday on November 13th, Sewek and Maryla give me my first sheets of letter-heading and envelopes with my mono-gram designed in gold (JcH). They make these at night while I am asleep. I remember wondering what to do with it. To whom should I write, and what about?

Meanwhile, new orders come thick and fast. In November 1941 any Aryan helping Jews, or any Jew leaving the ghetto without per-mission, is to be punished by death. From the 17th of December, the German post office refuses to accept mail out of the ghetto.

The texts on our cards get shorter. The only message they communicate now is that we are still alive and that we need food.

Card from Łucja to Mr Adam Berent, 49 Rua da Fonseca, Lisbon, Portugal, from Weinles Chaykin, Śliska 7, m.10, Warschau:

13 December 1941
> Kindly request you send us coffee, sardines, banacao and
> stock cubes for soup.
> Weinles Chaykin, Śliska 7, m.10, Warszawa

Card from Łucja to [Franciszka], addressed to Maria Werner, 49 da Fonseca, Lisbon, Portugal, from Ł. Weinles, Śliska 7, m.10, Warschau:

29 March 1942, received by Lisbon post office 15 April
> Dear Madame
> We have not heard from you for a month. Since the 9th
> of this month we have again received your gifts for which
> many thanks.
> Yours sincerely, Ł. Weinles, Maria Chaykin, Janina Chaykin

Card from Łucja and Maryla to Franka, addressed to Mme Marie Werner, 49 Rua da Fonseca, Lisbon, Portugal, from Maria Chaykin, Śliska 7, m.10, Warschau:

25 April 1942
> Chère Madame, please be so kind as to advise Mrs F. Themer-
> son that of late we have been receiving gifts all the time for

which we thank her and you very much, chère madame.

Yours sincerely Łucja Weinles, Maria Chaykin, Śliska 7/10

The tragedy of the Warsaw ghetto unfolds itself outside in the street. By spring 1942 I hardly ever leave our flat. Occasionally, shepherded by my mother, I do go out to walk round the block, but during these strolls she occasionally and without warning puts her hand over my eyes, protecting me from seeing atrocities that I could only guess at.

April is the beginning of the deportations from the ghetto. I still know nothing about it.

In 1963, Franciszka's school friend, Roma Elster, writes to tell her that she saw me frequently in the ghetto on ulica Sienna, and once being escorted by the police. She was obviously mistaken.

Card from Maryla to [Franka], addressed to Mme Maria Werner, 49 Rua da Fonseca, Lisbon, Portugal, from Maria Chaykin, Śliska 7, m.10, Warschau:

28 April 1942

Dear Madame, we are very grateful for frequent presents, sardines, almonds and figs. If it would be possible, we should be very grateful for cinnamon (canela), pepper and stock cubes. For further Liebesgabe we will be very grateful. Our best wishes and thanks to Mrs Themerson—Łucja Weinles, Maria Chaykin, Janina Chaykin

---

Card from Łucja to Franciszka, addressed to Mme Maria Werner (F. Themerson), 49 R. da Fonseca, Lisbon, Portugal, from Zofia Kolber, ul. Barokowa 2b m.2, Warszawa:

1 May 1942

Dear Madame, Thank you very much for such numerous presents, and we ask you kindly to continue to remember us. Please also convey our thanks and good wishes to Mrs Themerson. Please be kind enough to let her know that we are all in good health.

Yours sincerely, Ł. Weinles

Card from Łucja to Franciszka, addressed to Mme Maria Werner, 49 R. da Fonseca, Lisbon, Portugal, from Zofia Kolber, ul. Barokowa 2b m.2, Warszawa:

4 May 1942

My dearest, today we received your card from 14th April. We write very often. I thought that from Stefek there would also be a few words. My darling, I kiss you many times. We are all in good health. Jasia and her parents are well. Thank you very much for frequent greetings, news and parcels. Stefek's family is well. They work and send you best wishes. Mother is in good health.

Hugs from Ł. Weinles

The first organised actions, i.e. deportations, take place in May 1942.

Card from Łucja to Franciszka, addressed to Mme Maria Werner, 49 R. da Fonseca, Lisbon, Portugal, via Berlin, from Janina Plechawska, Barokowa 2b, m.2, Warschau, General Gouvernement:

28 May 1942

My darling Franeczko. We received your last three letters and I was upset that you haven't had news of your family for such a long time. We are all well, I and Maryla, Sewek and Jasia, also Stefek's family, mother, sister and brother-in-law, Anka. We receive constant help from daughter and sister and thanks to that we are managing. Sewek is working. Jasia is in good health.

Hugs and lots of kisses from Ł.W.

We had a card from Stefek.

Note: address via PCK or MOS London

Card from Łucja to Franciszka, addressed to Mme Maria Werner, 49 R. da Fonseca, Lisbon, Portugal, via Berlin, from Janina Plechawska, Barokowa 2b/2, Warschau, General Gouvernement:

28 May 1942, received by Lisbon post office 7 July 1942

Dear Madame, please be kind enough to advise Mrs F. Themerson that all her family: mother, sister, brother-in-law and Jasia are in good health, also Irena and her husband and mother, and all of them send her best wishes. We receive presents for which we are very grateful to you. Ł. Weinlesowa

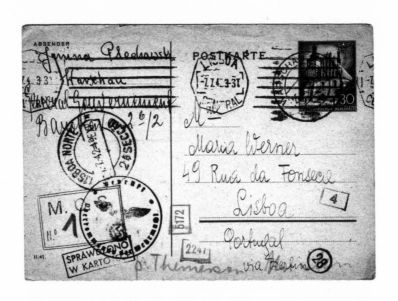

The penultimate card addressed by Maryla and written by Łucja

Last card from Łucja to Franciszka, addressed to Mme Maria Werner, 49 R. da Fonseca, Lisbon, Portugal, from Janina Plechawska, Barokowa 2b/2, Warschau, General Gouvernement:

20 June 1942, received by Lisbon post office 7 July 1942
    Dear Madame, would you be so very kind as to advise Mrs F. Themerson that her family: mother, sister, brother-in-law and Jasia are well and are sending her their best wishes and thank her for gifts. Irenka, Stefan and their mother are together and send their greetings. We ask for a reply.

Note: through PCK or MOS [Polish Red Cross or Ministry of Foreign Affairs]

This is the last missive from the ghetto. Franciszka, in London, working as she does for the Polish government-in-exile as a cartographer, has been aware of the situation in Warsaw. But in June 1942, the first public announcement about the Final Solution is made on the BBC.

On the day of that last missive of 20th June we are still together and still in Warsaw. But now I am about to leave.

From now on I shall start counting my journeys. The first journey was from ulica Piękna to the ghetto. Now I am getting ready for the second journey.

Twenty years later I shall receive, reading a letter from Halina Pągowska, now Czyżyńska, the unbearable news that the reason my father enters the ghetto from the relative safety of the outside is to arrange my escape. Maryla could not manage it alone. I don't know the precise date of my departure from the Warsaw ghetto, it must be sometime in June 1942, because on the 22nd of July the small ghetto will be surrounded and its liquidation begun. And I have no idea what plans my parents have in mind. For a couple of days there is a fluttering of nervousness in the ghetto. People come and go, talk in whispers, hurry hither and thither. Something is going to happen. Ludka, Heniek, and Wandzia are no longer around. I know nothing about their departure. Early one morning, my grandmother, my mother and I get into a rickshaw. Sewek, standing outside the entrance to our building, calls out to say good-bye. I rush back dutifully to kiss him. I don't manage to say good-bye. I can't say it. We ride to a hospital. There, my grandmother and I transfer to an ambulance. This is the only vehicle that can leave the ghetto unchallenged and possibly there is some payment made to the guards to facilitate our exit. Do I say good-bye to Maryla? No—there are no good-byes.

Why are my parents not travelling with us? Nobody tells me and I don't ask. There must be a reason. I have a feeling that they won't come. Only later do I allow myself to think that perhaps there wasn't enough money, contacts, influence, luck for us all to leave together. For now, I concentrate on the journey. The ambulance is full. I sit next to my grandmother on a narrow bench covered with torn black plastic.

We travel to Zofiówka in Otwock, the hospital for the mentally ill run by Irena and Stefan Miller, which I had visited so many times throughout my life. Zofiówka isn't just a hospital, it is a large estate with many buildings, fields, woods, gardens. This large parkland is now a ghetto too. I am trying to think by what means the enclosure is separated from the rest of Otwock, but all I remember is some barbed wire that I will eventually have to climb through. Irena and Stefan Miller are not there, but other members of the family are present: Irena's mother, Salomea Themerson; my grandmother Łucja's brother, Władek; also some friends and acquaintances. A teacher is soon found and I attend classes with three or four other girls of my age. I recall nothing about those lessons but what I do remember clearly are the lessons I have with my grandmother. I learn about God, the Holy Ghost, Mary, and Jesus. I learn Catholic prayers in Polish and in Latin, the catechism, stories from the New Testament, lives of the principal saints. I no longer ask my grandmother if all this means anything to her, and I don't know what it means to me except that it is my passport to the future.

I want to go back to my parents. My grandmother explains that the Warsaw ghetto will soon be liquidated, perhaps within days. There is an ambulance going back to Warsaw, and I can go if I really want to. Was there a moment of indecision? I don't remember because I have already discovered a method, or principle for making important decisions. I would ask myself the question: what do my parents want me to do? and then act accordingly. Do I know now that I will never see my parents again? I don't and can't ask myself such a question.

And so I don't return to Warsaw but stay with my grandmother in Zofiówka; not for very long, a few days, perhaps another week. My education in the Catholic faith continues. My next escape is on the cards but again nothing is said. I am merely aware that there will be another journey. Nothing is discussed in front of me and this is helpful, since I don't have to worry in advance.

I live from day to day. I am still more or less at home. People around me are nice to each other. Stefan Themerson's mother teaches me embroidery. I go for walks, pick flowers, play ball with my friends. During the following three days, however, I guess that our ghetto too will not continue for much longer. I have no recollection of what my grandmother tells me but one day I just simply know that the time is fast approaching for me to leave. A couple more walks, a visit to the kiosk to buy sweets, permission from Stefan's mother to pick a couple of sunflowers even though they are not quite ready. Łucja sews a couple of silver coins into my blouse. In another seam is a list of addresses. I take with me a round silver brooch with cut out enamelled daisies and, quite recklessly, a photograph of my grandmother. I will lose both of them within days. The decision to leave is my own. Of the three possible options remaining to me, one is now out of the question: it is already too late to return to the Warsaw ghetto with the ambulance. The two that are left are to stay with my grandmother, or to leave. I imagine that some payment has been made to a family outside the Otwock ghetto to take care of me. I suppose that the Bechstein grand has been sold principally for that purpose. Which means, of course, that leaving is what my parents want me to do. Doubts evaporate. I shall go. Yes, I am frightened, I don't really know what I am doing, but I shall go. Simultaneously, I begin to suspect—in fact I become convinced—that my grandmother and her brother are going to commit suicide. I look at the elegant carafe on the round table covered with a white tablecloth in the sitting room. The carafe is covered with a white lace napkin and I imagine that it contains the poison that they will swallow. Of course, nothing is said. In reality, I didn't know what means they would use to end their lives, but eventually I do find out that they committed suicide by taking cyanide.

The Warsaw ghetto, the so-called small ghetto, is finally liquidated on 10th August 1942. The Otwock ghetto is liquidated on 19th August. Most of the residents are either shot or are sent to Treblinka. Stefan Themerson's mother and all the others perish. Stefan and Irena Miller are killed by the guides that were meant to be taking them across the border. My parents are deported from the Warsaw ghetto to Treblinka, in the autumn, or perhaps in November. I learn eventually that they are among the last to be taken, having worked in the German workshops.

I leave Zofiówka, according to the instructions from my grandmother. Again, there are no good-byes, no last words of advice. I am now in charge of my own life. This is the first time I set out alone to go anywhere, but my usual fear evaporates. At nightfall I proceed to the edge of a wood, climb under some barbed wire using sticks to prop it up, and walk right through the wood to the other side, changing directions several times according to grandmother's instructions. I have been told to walk purposefully but not to approach my destination in a straight line. Today I cannot imagine how long it took, perhaps twenty minutes, perhaps a little longer. At the other end, a man is standing against a tree quietly whistling to himself. He greets me and without further ado takes me to his house. Apart from his wife, there are several other children. Each child has a corner of the sitting room, I occupy half a sofa and this is where I sit and sleep for two nights and two days. This is my third journey since life was normal, and the first one undertaken by myself.

The following day I am sent out to get some water from a pump in the village square. As I am pumping the water, a young child, a girl, walks up to me with a challenge: 'Cross yourself!', she commands. 'You shouldn't take God's name in vain', I retort without even thinking. My grandmother's lessons are effective. I know immediately that the girl was sent to the pump by her parents and I become worried. When I return to the house, I relate my 'adventure'; my 'caretakers' congratulate me on my clever reply and appear both pleased and entertained by the event.

Who are my 'caretakers'? I never learn their names. I'm not sure how long I am supposed to stay with them, don't know what sort of an arrangement was made on my behalf, and don't dare ask. Above all, I don't feel safe. I decide to leave. During my last day there, some of the money sewn into my blouse by my grandmother is spent on a trip to a village shop with the other children, to buy sweets—or should I say, to buy their friendship, to have some moments of pleasure with my contemporaries. Are they also hiding? Are they Jewish? I never find out. Nor do I want to. This is not a time for asking questions. I must be careful what I say. There are many safe subjects of conversation available: nature, the weather, saint days, the colour of potatoes. Subjects one doesn't speak about are Germans, Jews, the ghetto, food, money, neighbours, relatives, and various other basic things.

I ask my hosts if they could arrange for me to get to an address in Warsaw. They agree immediately and suggest that one of their friends who is going to Warsaw by train might be able to deliver me to one of the addresses on my list. This is the address of Ludka and Wandzia, who shared our flat in the Warsaw ghetto, which is where I last saw them. They succeeded in getting out in good time. On this, my fourth journey to Warsaw, I am accompanied by a kind and civilised man who delivers me to their doorstep. I ring the bell. He waits until the door opens and I am ushered in. Their pleasure in seeing me is quite obviously mixed with surprise and consternation. They are staying in somebody's apartment. My presence can cause problems and endanger us all. Being with them is like being at home once more. We have supper together, I am found a place to sleep. But this, alas, cannot last for very long. It is decided that I have to try my luck elsewhere and go to another address on my list. The following morning Wandzia takes me on my fifth journey to a bus or a tram terminus on Koło, very close to the home of my father's colleague, the architect Halina Pągowska. We arrive at the terminus, and now the plan is that I go and look for Halina's house while Wandzia waits to make sure that I can find it. I do find the house and ring the bell. The door is opened by an older woman than the one I expect to see. I ask for Halina Pągowska and am told that she is out. A moment of panic. I tell the elderly lady that I will come back and rush back to the bus terminus, only to find that Wandzia is no longer there. Another moment of panic. How could members of my own family send me away to try my luck elsewhere and not even wait long enough to find out if I was successful? But there was no time to think. Once more to Halina's house. I ring the bell and Halina herself comes to the door. 'I am the daughter of Seweryn Chaykin', I blurt out. Without a word, she lets me in.

Halina lives in a white bungalow in a suburban district of Warsaw with two baby sons and her mother. For the next week or perhaps just a few days she looks after me like a member of her own family. It is not easy. She is risking her life for me. Am I aware of the danger my presence entails for her family? The house is a bungalow, with windows all around. Nobody must see me. Neighbours are nosey and even a three-year-old boy could say something about a new person staying in the house. I sleep on an iron bedstead. My hair ribbon is wound around the bed frame to straighten it. It is still important that the ribbon should look ironed. Much of the day is spent under this same bedstead, in a cupboard, or in the lavatory. The family cannot risk my being seen through any of the windows or by anyone visiting the house, not even, or perhaps especially, the children's friends. I can feel that Halina is nervous about my presence. And yes, I have heard that there is a death penalty for hiding Jews, and when at the end of a short time, perhaps two or three days, Halina tells me that she is going to take me to my father's office, I welcome the news. Again, the journey has to be planned very precisely. I am to proceed to a bus stop by myself and take the bus. Halina will get on the same bus at the following stop. When we arrive at our destination, I am to follow her at some distance, pretending, of course, that we don't know each other. Before leaving the house, she advises me not to smile because smiling emphasises my semitic features. I try to remember this instruction since it is bound to be useful later. I shall smile at night when nobody is looking. Meanwhile, I daren't even think what would happen should I get lost.

This bus journey is the sixth journey and it goes without any difficulties. I get on the bus. Take care not to look at anyone, stare out of the window, and count the bus stops to make sure I get out at the right one in case I don't see Halina. We arrive at my father's office, which I had never visited before. This is a large architectural practice concerned with social housing in the Warsaw district of Koło. It is here that I am given a new identity, new papers, a new surname. Once more the surname begins with the letter C, Cegłowska, in case somewhere among my few belongings there is a monogram. The surname's suffix, *ska*, indicates Polish provenance. The first two syllables refer to the word 'brick'. Is this name selected because my father's colleagues are architects? The day spent in my father's office is the most comforting of my entire wartime experience. I meet several of my father's colleagues, and since we are upstairs and no strangers can come in, I need neither hide nor pretend. I am longing to talk, to unburden myself, to mention my parents. My seventh journey starts there. That evening, I am escorted by another of my father's colleagues to her flat in Bielany. I am sad to have forgotten her name, all the more so since I would see her several times during the following two months. I stay with her in Bielany for two or three days. The flat is high above the street, she lives alone, and I don't have to hide during the day. I read, and now and then rush into the kitchen where there is a saucepan of cabbage cooked with tomatoes. I eat whenever there is an opportunity and anyway, I am always hungry. What is important is that nobody can see me through the windows.

Eventually, my father's colleagues decide that the safest place for me would be a hospital. And so my eighth journey takes me to a children's ward of a general hospital where I have to pretend to be ill. My acting is convincing enough for me to be admitted and kept, fed and given medicines. I make friends with other children, help out on the ward, and gradually fall genuinely ill with chicken- pox. The friend from Bielany visits me, she combs and plaits my hair and brings me presents. After a month, the ward sister comes to the obvious conclusion that nobody is going to collect me and that I have no home. And so on my ninth journey, I am sent to an orphanage.

No questions are asked, no explanations are necessary. I have no decisions to make. So long as I am in an institution there seems to be no danger. Danger exists outside, in the street. While being escorted to the orphanage by a sister from the hospital, and while we are waiting for a tram, I am approached by two official looking men and asked my name. 'Maria Cegłowska', I say. Then, I am asked for my mother's maiden name. I say: 'Kwiatkowska'. Then my grandfather's Christian name, I say 'Józef'. The men leave. Later, I wonder whether I had said 'Kwiatkowska' or 'Kwiecińska', but it no longer matters, and I am never asked this question again. How to invent names to prevent anyone of suspecting me of being Jewish? For a surname, choose some innocent noun without any specific associations, e.g., 'Kwiat', flower, and add the appropriate suffix. When selecting a first name, make sure it is as close to Jesus as possible, thus 'Joseph' for a man and 'Maria' for a woman; 'Jan' is good and so are 'Teresa' and 'Anna'.

The orphanage is big. Boys and girls sleep in large dormitories. There is no organised routine because new children arrive daily.

We are stripped, cleaned, disinfected, inoculated, examined for lice. I remember the surprise of the staff that with my thick long hair I had no lice. The orphanage is a staging post and my stay here is very short, a few days. I am relieved when the time comes to move once again. The reason for my relief is this: at night, when the lights are out, I tell stories to the other children in the dormitory. Or, rather, a single story over several episodes. The story is about my father, an engineer and architect, who with his brave and ingenious colleagues is building an underground passageway under the city. The purpose of all this is to rescue us from the orphanage and to take us to some unidentified but lovely place in the country. There are some twenty or so children in the dormitory and some of them keep on asking me for progress reports of this rescue mission. Where did I think my father had got to. I invent obstacles, heroic deeds, floods, the necessity to rescue zoo animals first. I make the mistake of pointing to a place in the centre of the floor through which the rescue party is meant to emerge. The following day two boys are lying on the floor with their ears to the ground on the very spot I had indicated, but that, luckily, is the day I leave.

The stay at the orphanage is temporary for everyone. All the children are gradually allocated to convents and institutions in different parts of Poland. As my luck would have it, and it really couldn't be worse, I am sent to Otwock. But there is nothing to be done. I pretend, of course, that I had never been there before. 'Otwock, where is that?' There are three of us, girls, travelling together by train, on this my tenth journey. Before we leave, my friend from Bielany appears at the railway station to say good-bye. She hands me a large tin of Ovaltine. It will last me for two weeks.

The convent in Otwock is run by nuns who wear ordinary clothes, Sisters of the Disrobed Pure Heart of Mary; I think that this was the name of the convent. We arrive at a large two-storey wooden villa, somewhat yellow in colour, with a large attic. The daily activities of the boys and girls—there about twenty of us—include work in the kitchen, mostly peeling potatoes and slicing cabbage; making slippers out of felt; and a great deal of cleaning, polishing, and washing. The dormitories are in another building near by. Occasionally there is the sound of gunfire in the distance. I try to ignore it. There are no lessons that I recall but we sing and pray much of the time. But I also go for short walks, play ball, make drawings, and read whatever is available. We sing popular songs about a highlander who left home ('Góralu czy ci nie żal?'), about my rosemary growing ('O mój rozmarynie rozwijaj się'), about your going through the mountain while I go through the valley ('Ty pójdziesz górą, ty pójdziesz górą a ja doliną . . .'), and about a little red apple cut into quarters ('Czerwone jabłuszko przekrojone na krzyż').

Every day after a lunch consisting of 'żurek' (a watery soup with a piece of potato floating in the middle), all the children sit around a long table with their heads on their arms. This is a rest period. One day, a nun motions to me and another girl to follow her. She takes us upstairs and locks us in the attic. Minutes later Gestapo officers arrive to inspect the convent.

They don't come upstairs. As soon as they leave, we are fetched to join the others.

Within three months my head is alive with lice; it starts after we spend half a day jumping and rolling down a couple of haystacks. One morning, some weeks later, I sit on the veranda with a towel round my shoulders while one of the nuns cuts off my plait. It is long—my hair has never been cut. This has to be done because my scalp is covered in sores. The plait is tied with a ribbon at both ends and given to me as a souvenir. I will keep it under my pillow. I don't really want it, but since it was given to me, I accept it politely. My head is entirely shaved with the exception of a pointed tuft above my forehead. I am lucky, there are no mirrors. Subsequently I develop a high fever, and when I am better, Sister Czesława tells me that I am going to be christened. I often wonder what I unwittingly revealed during my illness. But no revelations are needed: of course the sisters know who is who. One day when the girls are dressed in white to attend their first communion and I want to join them, Sister Czesława stops me from following them and says that time has not yet come for me to go to my first communion. I have to be christened first. And indeed this is what now happens. She is my godmother, and the priest, whose name I forget, is my godfather. I choose my names: Maria Janina Teresa—the most Catholic names I can think of. Only the middle name has any connection with my original identity, and I am glad that Jan, or St John the Baptist, features in the New Testament as the very saint involved with the christening ritual.

Christening picture with a note from my godmother.

Soon after I go to my first communion, in a white dress like other girls, and am given another souvenir with a message, dated 12 January 1943:

I enjoy going to church and the chapel. The music is always beautiful and so is the singing. I get used to praying. I pray in Latin and find comfort in the communal spirit of reciting and repeating the words together. Praying is restful and quiet; all you hear is the shimmering sound of voices, and you can think about whatever you like.

At night, once again, I tell stories to other children, but now they have a religious and fabulous flavour. I don't mention my family. The stories are usually about children befriended by animals, animals being rescued by Jesus, and so on. Rescue still continues to be a major topic. God is ever present. I don't know how each of the stories will end. They just continue and one adventure leads to another.

On my real birthday (my identity papers give a different day) I hide myself in a lavatory to weep. This occasional outlet for my feelings has to be planned in advance. I have to make sure that nobody is likely to be around. Once the coast is clear I lock myself in the farthest lavatory, think of my parents, and howl passionately. When I am discovered on one of these occasions I excuse my outburst by saying that today is my mother's birthday. The sister who finds me tries to console me saying that now it is the Mother of God who is my mother. Yes, I am grateful to the Mother of God, I am grateful to the sister who tries to console me, but my problem is insoluble. I know too much, and I am alone.

Sometimes when the children leave the precincts of the convent I am left behind. The ostensible reason is that I must perform some special task, make decorations for the Christmas tree, or draw something. I draw, cut and glue pieces of coloured paper and when the others return they help me. Christmas comes and goes, snow falls and melts. Spring comes and then summer and all the time I am getting more and more ill. My legs are covered with sores, so is my scalp, and there is nothing that the Otwock nuns can do to help me. There is no medicine and our diet is minimal. No amount of gherkins pinched at night from a large barrel in the kitchen, no amount of sucking nasturtium blooms can make up for lack of food. The sisters decide to take me to a hospital in Warsaw.

Before I leave, Sister Czesława gives me another souvenir on 12 February 1944:

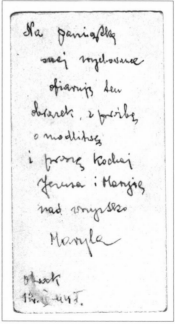

And so, one morning, Sister Janina accompanies me to Warsaw by train on my eleventh journey. I don't know exactly where she is taking me. It is short walk from the station. We walk up the wide shallow steps up to the gate of the convent of the Franciscan Sisters of the Family of Mary. Sister Janina asks me to sit down on the top step and wait. She rings the bell. Before I know what has happened, she bolts. I am alone on the doorstep and the door remains closed. Another moment of panic. A minute later, it cannot be more than that, a nun opens the door, takes one look at me, and takes me in. She is wearing a black habit and a stiff, round, white collar. On her head, beyond a white rim around the forehead, a long black veil. With every movement, she makes a rustling sound. All that cloth around her. She is somewhere inside it. I only see the face—a pale oval with indistinct features. I overhear her telling someone that another child has been abandoned on the doorstep. She points to a small stool by the door. I sit down. Within minutes three nuns march down the corridor toward me. One of them peers down at me carefully. She makes a gesture with her hand and points to a door in the distance. It must be a clinic. I get up and follow her. So many things happen, so many steps are negotiated without use of words. Once more I don't need to say anything, in this instance I just have to give my name: Maria Cegłowska. I accept the events as they unveil themselves in front of me. So far so good. I am taken to what is virtually a hospital ward, put in a clean bed, smeared all over with pungent yellow ointment, and bandaged. I am fed several times a day and within a week am well enough to start taking interest in what is happening around me. The full cure takes several weeks. There are books to read and coloured crayons and paper. As I am discharged from the hospital one of the nuns notices that I have managed to pack a book[4] in my bag as well as some crayons. I protest when I'm asked to give them back but they are taken away from me anyway. The nun doesn't realise of course that I am really, truly, the appropriate owner of such things: that I need them. This, however, is a minor setback; I am healthy, my skin has healed even though some residual marks will stay with me for the rest of my life.

For my twelfth journey I am admitted to the convent school in Warsaw run by the same nuns as the hospital. It is in the same building, or an annex. All the girls wear uniforms: white blouses and navy blue tunics. We sleep in a dormitory, perhaps twenty of us. We wear long cotton night-dresses. In the morning we wash in a communal washroom at long metal sinks. This has to be done very carefully without undressing. The body is never seen. When I develop an abscess in my right armpit, it takes me a couple of weeks before I dare tell the nun in charge of our dorm about it and receive treatment.

There are regular classes. I continue to take my religion seriously and write essays about saints which are well received by the teachers. My efforts are appreciated and this encourages me to continue. When my store of information about real saints becomes depleted, I invent some minor saintly persons, all of whom have suffered, have overcome difficulties, and are eventually duly rewarded. The pattern of these stories is familiar and comforting. They are about positive resolution to pain and martyrdom:

4 *Panna z mokrą głową* by Kornel Makuszyński

a satisfactory ending. Either the protagonists become saints, or God acknowledges their efforts and sends them some deserved recompense in this life. All of which is quite logical; I can think up any number of stories that fit such a scheme. There is, however, a minor problem. Religion is a part of my life here and now, but it wasn't always. I write about a heaven which despite my conversion to Catholicism I don't believe in. I don't believe that my parents are in any of the three available destinations— hell, purgatory, or heaven—and therefore these places cannot exist. I know that my parents are dead although nobody has actually told me that this is the case. Where are they? They are nowhere, but they exist somehow because I feel that they continue to look after me. In my imagination they seem to tell me what to do, what to say, and how to behave.

The convent school has some day pupils, and one Sunday I am allowed to accompany one of the girls to her mother for tea. For the occasion, I am dressed in a pale-blue cord dress with a large white collar. My hair has grown by now and when I look in the mirror I am surprised to recognise my old self. I am pleased. My friend and I go to her home. This is a normal home, with pictures on the walls, a table with a tablecloth, porcelain cups and saucers, napkins, a vase with flowers, chairs with leather seats; there is a cake for tea. In the hall there is a bookcase filled with books. My friend's mother is upset to see me—such a well-brought-up girl—an orphan in a convent. Her comments make me feel embarrassed. I don't see myself in that light at all. I don't think of myself as an orphan: orphans are invariably poor, unhappy, and thin. I am not poor or thin, and only sometimes sad. I am merely a sort of Cinderella going through the necessary initiation rituals. Do I think of the future? Perhaps a week ahead, no more—but I do tell the nuns that I intend to become a Mother Superior. Of course, I don't mention the fact that I never intend to do novitiate or become an ordinary nun.

When the convent is shelled and starts burning we all escape into the street. Some of us rush into the nearest church. I hide under the altar, assuming that this is the safest place. There is more shelling, more fire, several casualties. I don't know who dies or who is wounded. Within hours, the nuns collect those of us who survive and shepherd us out of the city. There are about twenty of us, all girls of different ages; they will be my companions for the year to come.

How we make this, my thirteenth journey, I have no recollection, but I expect that it is in a van commandeered from somewhere by the Mother Superior. We arrive in Pustelnik II. It is a village. We find ourselves in a smaller branch of the Franciscan Sisters of the Family of Mary convent requisitioned to take in the Warsaw survivors. There is no school. Accommodation is ad hoc. By then I have enough experience in fitting in, being helpful, and saying things that please. I offer prayers for a nun that is ill, for a child injured in the Warsaw church. I give thanks to God, selected saints, and the bravest nuns. One of the sisters, Sister Salomea, has a broken right arm. I decide to be her assistant and spend my time helping her. By now I also know how to clean, polish, wash linen, do simple sewing, and peel potatoes at great speed.

I am given privileges. While other children are left to do house-work, I am given an orchard to look after and a dog to keep me company. Every morning the dog and I, with a packet of sandwiches, walk to the orchard and stay there all day. The orchard is small. There are apple trees and pear trees. There is also a shed with some old books. I play with the dog, eat a few apples, and read whatever I can find. Occasionally, five or six of us are sent to help in a Polish soldiers' camp in the vicinity. For our work peeling vegetables, cooking, and washing-up, we are given a cooked meal. The food is much better than anything any of us have eaten for a long time.

We spend time playing ball, singing, and gardening. I do this with other girls and the atmosphere is friendly but we don't talk about anything that matters. Nobody talks about parents or where we lived before the war. Each one of us has a past which is never broached. Perhaps this is the reason I don't have any especially close friends among the girls, although I enjoy all social activities. There are so many things we can talk about that don't matter that the absence of personal details or confidences is not noticeable. We all look vaguely similar, navy blue tunic, white blouse, and most of us have plaits.

One day, we are all given written tests to see who is up to standard to go to a school in the nearest town, half an hour away by train. Most of the girls are older and join the second year. I am the youngest and am accepted for the first. I enjoy school, sitting in a real classroom with different teachers for a variety of subjects. French is my favourite subject; I still remember some of the lessons I had with Mme Jacob back in the ghetto. Getting to school is a problem. None of us have money to buy train tickets, but our presence on the train every day is more or less ignored. On one occasion the conductor does come and demands to see our tickets. To this day I am embarrassed to remember rising, drawing myself up to my full height and shouting at him: 'Do you want Polish children to go about without shoes?' He too is embarrassed and leaves us alone, and we are never bothered again.

It must already be the summer of 1945 when we are all given medical examinations, and a young woman psychologist comes to the convent to assess the girls. It is not clear why, but it might have had something to do with possible adoptions, or a survey. Each one of us is called into a room in turn. For one of the tests we are required to draw a picture. My pencil drawing is of a woman in a long coat and a hat walking along a path with a small dog. After looking at it carefully, the psychologist says: 'This looks like the drawings of Maryla Chaykin.' 'That's my mother', I say.

This admission is a mistake, the words just slipped out; it was just so nice to hear someone say my mother's name. Anyway, the war is over, I should be able to reveal my identity. That evening Sister Joanna gives me a beating with a leather belt for concealing my background. Apart from that nothing happens. I continue at school, pray, attend church, and watch the orchard at weekends. When a boy from my class comes to fetch me on his bicycle to take me to school, the nuns don't permit me to accompany him and send him away, much to my distress. I am only eleven but I am very attracted to this tall blond boy called Jaś who is in the form above me.

•

In August 1945, Franciszka writes countless letters to the Red Cross and all possible contacts in Poland to see if anyone of her family has survived. Some of the letters are returned when they don't reach their destination. One of them is sent to the Administration of ul. Piusa XI 25. The letter is returned with a note dated 28 August, saying: 'the building on Piusa XI has burnt down'.

This is one of Franciszka's letters:

Dear Sir,
Would you be so kind as to let me know whether you are in contact or if you have any information of your former tenants of flat no.12 in house no.25 on ul. Piusa XI—engineer Seweryn Chaykin, his wife Marja and daughter Janina. They lived in this flat from 1929 to the autumn of 1940. I should be grateful for the quickest reply.
I enclose an international postal coupon and thank you in advance.
Yours faithfully,
Franciszka Themerson

Another letter from Franciszka to Zofja Kolber, ul. Barakowa nr.2b, m.2, Warszawa:

10 August 1945

Dear Mrs Kolber,

I should be grateful if you would kindly let me know if you have any news whatever about my mother, Łucja Weinles, my sister Marja Chaykin and her husband Seweryn Chaykin and daughter, Jasia, who lived on ul. Śliska 7, m.10.

I am writing to you about this because I once received a card from them to Lisbon with your return address.

Thanking you in advance, I enclose an international reply coupon asking you for a quickest reply.

Respectfully yours

Franciszka Themerson

The letter is returned with the message 'Retour—maison brûlée'.

Letter from Ludka Haller Sobieralska in Sierpc, H. Haller Sobieralski, Starosta powiatowy, Sierpc, to Franciszka & Stefan, 49 Randolph Avenue, London W9:

26 October 1945

My Dearest Ones!

At last, Wandzia, while she was in Warsaw, found your address and I hasten to write a few words. Unfortunately I can't send you any good news: we are alive, the four of us and Jasia, but so far I don't know where she is. I am looking for her. She was placed in September/October 1942 in a convent in Otwock, but she is no longer in any of the convents there. I am doing what I can, it is very much weighing on my conscience. Her surname is Cegłowska.

Warm kisses

Meanwhile, all sorts of people come to our convent to visit. Girls stand in groups, some are brought forward and introduced. The purpose of all this is adoption. Some girls long to be adopted and stand about smiling charmingly. I sit at the back and am lucky not to be pushed forward during these rituals. I don't want to go anywhere. I am happy going to school and tending the orchard.

My French teacher at school finds an advertisement searching for me in a newspaper and alerts the nuns. The nuns contact the Haller Sobieralskis, who placed it. The following day, Heniek and Wandzia come with a car to fetch me. Heniek is now a mayor of a small town, Sierpc. The nuns give me some clothes which are to be returned in due course. I pack my few belongings and we leave. However happy I am to see them, I don't really want to leave. My life in the convent has a comfortable routine, I like the school, and I can't face any more changes, or 'journeys' as I always call them.

Ludka, Wandzia, and Heniek Haller
Sobieralski, 1945

And so my fourteenth journey is to Sierpc, a small town north
of Warsaw, where Henryk is mayor. Once there, I realise that it's
lovely to be back with my family. There are lots of books, a new
school, Wandzia is teaching me to jive and to knit, and there is
a dog called Rex to play with. To begin with, I spend most of
my time reading: *The Iliad*, *The Odyssey*, Sienkiewicz, Norwid,
Mickiewicz. Ludka will soon complain that I read too much.

On 9th November 1945, Ludka writes to the Themersons:

> My Dears! At last I have Jasia. She looks well, feels well and
> is somewhat dazed, because in the course of a single day

she changed her environment. On Monday she will start school, because they must find a place if it is for the mayor. Wandzia now has her own sister and treats her very well, so does Heniek, who shows her a lot of tenderness, like a father. I can't write any more before I get a letter from you, or perhaps we shall see you soon.

I kiss you a lot,
Ludka

Ludka's letter is accompanied by my drawings and on the other side are two letters from me:

Dearest Franiu!!!

I miss you very much. I have been found and am with Auntie Ludka and I am happy. I was in all sorts of places and circumstances but all that is over. I am very pleased that in London you didn't live through the same experiences. I should very much like to see you and I am interested to know if you have changed. I attend the first class in the gimnazjum [secondary school]. I can't play the piano anymore because for 3½ years I didn't play at all, but I have not forgotten how to draw. You probably draw all the time as before. Franiu, if you were able to and there is ever a chance, do come to us.

Jasia Cegłowska

Dearest Stefek,

How long it is since I last saw you. How is your health, how are you? For me everything is over. Are you still making films and writing poems. Is the little book about a pig published? I probably won't recognise you as we haven't seen each other for such a long time. I think about you always and from time to time I dream about you.

I finish this letter with a thousand kisses.

Jasia Cegłowska

In Sierpc there is a sense of excitement in the air. People come and go, the house is busy. It is, after all, the house of a mayor. Domestic activities at home are a new pleasure. I help with cooking. Ludka and Heniek are surprised that I am neither shy nor fearful and take everything for granted. I am busy helping Wandzia to choose between two suitors, and am making new friends. Life slips into a new routine. We are in touch with Franciszka and Stefan in London, and I am trying to anticipate the next change that awaits me when I shall join them. It will still be three more months. The move to London is far from simple. It is assumed, and by me too, that I shall go to London. Efforts to obtain a visa for me and a seat on a plane are already in hand, but there are complications and a great many important people waiting for a flight allocation to London. Several of the Themersons' friends are recruited to help, among them: Jerzy Michałowski, a former colleague of my father's at TOR, and Roman Piotrowski and his wife Marysia, who will be involved in helping to sort out the endless formalities for my departure for London.

Meanwhile, I write to my godmother in Otwock to tell her that I survived and found my family. She responds, but when I write once again my letter goes astray. This time I have to address the envelope by myself and don't know how to do it.

I write to Franka and Stefan:

Dearest Franka and Stefan,

Today we received your letter. It made me very happy. I can't wait for the moment when I can see you. I don't know English, not a word, and I don't know what's going to happen about that. If I were to leave during the school year, then I must try to get a certificate that I completed the 1st class of gimnazjum. Are there Polish schools? If it wasn't for the fact that you are there, I wouldn't want to go to England. Are there many Poles there? I can't imagine that I will be travelling by air. Franka, have you changed a lot, will I recognise you? I can't wait for the moment when I will greet you. I have grown very little, that will

129

probably surprise you. Write and tell me if you can where is Paweł.

Lots of kisses and till I see you soon!

Jasia—'Jack-of-all-trades'!

Paweł, Sewek's youngest brother, is in Italy. His journey took him from Lwów to Russia, to Siberia, to Persia, and, with the army of General Anders, to Monte Cassino, Bari, and in 1947 to Foxley Camp in Hereford.

Paweł in Bari, 1946

I regale my school friends with stories about England, all of them invented since I really know nothing about it. Franciszka describes London to me in her letters. She explains that it consists of towns joined together, each one with its own name and its own town hall; that there is one area with large department stores, another with the editorial offices of newspapers. She assures me that English people are very nice.

Franciszka sends me a blue woollen skirt with shoulder straps, two pullovers, a scarf, and underwear. She hopes that they are not too small for me but it is just the opposite, they are too big. I wonder now if I will recognise them, do they have white hair? Do they keep any animals in their house? Is there a decorated Christmas tree? I thought that after Christmas I wouldn't go to school in Poland anymore, but it is already January and I have to return to my classes once more.

When I arrive in Warsaw on Friday, 25th January 1946, starting on my fifteenth journey to London, the city is a terrible shock. It is completely demolished. I could not have imagined anything like it, and I try not to look. Seeing Warsaw in ruins is a shocking experience.

I carry a small brown plastic suitcase, the likes of which are to be found in every play about refugees. In it are the souvenirs of some of my journeys and presents for Franka and Stefan from Ludka and family. I wear a brown wool coat with a hood and a small fur collar. These are specially made for my departure. I imagine that they must be elegant, although I soon see that they are not.

I spend a night in Warsaw with Lonia Janecka, a painter friend of Franciszka from the Academy of Fine Arts. Her flat is really the home of an artist, it has the familiar smell of oil paint. It is a studio. She has a radio that stuns me like a revelation with its myriad new possibilities. It is a revelation, and I can barely hold a conversation, I am so excited about listening to it. From then on she will call me 'my friend of the radio'.

My passport photograph, December 1945

The journey to London takes two days with a night spent in the Berlin airport. I arrive on the 28th of January 1946 at RAF Blackbushe Airport. The journey and the arrival are described in my and Franciszka's letters.

My letter to Ludka, Heniek, and Wandzia after my arrival in London on 30th January:

My dearest ones,

I am already here. I arrived on Monday. On Saturday there was fog over London so our departure was put off till Sunday. We all arrived at Polonia and from there went to the airport by car, where our suitcases were examined. Afterwards, Lonia Janecka escorted me to the airplane and we took off. I didn't feel very well during the flight. After 2½ hours we landed in an airport near Berlin where we spent the night. Anna Fidler, who accompanied me, gave me pills to make me feel better during the next stage of the journey. Next day at 8 in the morning we took off for England. I was looking out of the window the entire time and saw everything, even the boats on the water. The rest of the journey took 5¾ hours and I was very tired. At the airport in England once more we had to go from one office to another, and then a bus to London. In town, Stefek and Franka were already waiting for me and we kissed endlessly. We have many Polish friends in London, who are also delighted that I came. There are double-decker buses here, but practically no trams. We live in a lovely house on the 3rd floor. We have 4 rooms, a large bathroom, kitchen, stairs in the apartment, and corridors. English people, from the very first moment, made a very nice impression on me. Now I am tidying up everything. Franka looks terribly thin. I have already made the acquaintance of all sorts of dogs in the street. Now I am walking about everywhere looking at everything. Wandzia, please write to tell me about your choice, won't you? and about Rex, has he been found? Good-bye for now! and a thousand kisses—

    Jasia

In the same letter to which I added the above, Franciszka wrote that it was a pity that they couldn't have witnessed my leave-taking of the other people on the flight. The pilot had kissed my hand, I kissed all the others, and they promised to visit me. The number of times I kiss Franka and Stefek are counted to begin with, but the counting is soon given up. The moment we arrive, I start organising everything, I tell everyone to switch off the lights on leaving a room, insist that Franka eats, and set about making order. Franka and Stefan are so happy to have me with them that they put up with my impossible behaviour. I am the centre of the world and am putting the world to rights. Within four months of leaving Pustelnik I have changed from a prag-matic, well-behaved child into a problem.

•

49 Randolph Avenue, my new home, is a large stucco building forming part of a terrace. The building has a porch with col-umns and a black front door. To reach the flat, we climb the

green carpeted staircase to the third floor. The Themersons' maisonette on the 3rd and 4th floors is unlike anything that I am used to. First of all, it is fairly bare. Secondly, for the first time in my life, I have a room to myself. I don't like it. I am used to the constant presence of others and it takes me some time to get used to it. I make paper cut-outs to stick on the window of my room and attach silver circles from sweet wrappers all over the pale grey walls. The room very gradually becomes my own, but it takes a while.

My behaviour in these new circumstances is altogether inappropriate. I cut up Franka's best drawing paper to make a tutu for myself. I am demanding and bossy, expect constant company and attention. I take over the house, clean, organise, and complain. This may be a way of making myself at home, but for Franciszka and Stefan my presence must have been a greater shock than anything they might have expected. This new family unit of three people shaken by war does not come about easily.

Here is what the apartment looks like. When you reach the third floor, the entrance hall is wide and shallow. My room is on the right. It has a Picasso reproduction in a white frame, two drawings by Franka, and a gouache by Peter Potworowski, who presented it to me as a gift on my arrival. The subject of this picture is Golgotha and I wonder why he thinks it appropriate. Luckily, I am familiar with the subject. The walls are painted light grey. I have a bed with a blue hessian cover, white bookshelves, a small desk painted black, and a built-in cupboard. There is a stool, a side table, and an easy chair. Next door is Franka and Stefan's

135

bedroom, which doubles as an office. Opposite the entrance to the flat is a large empty bathroom. On the left of the entrance is the kitchen. One wall is grey, one white, and one pink. There is a group of thin horizontal pipes lining the grey right-hand wall that are painted in different pastel shades. They are absolutely lovely. There is a grey sideboard, a round table, a sink with cold water, and a gas cooker. Upstairs are Stefan's study and Franka's studio. The stairs are covered with thick felt with canvas on top, on which Franka and Stefan made black imprints of their hands and feet. The floors are painted black. Furniture is rudimentary and is either painted black or is bare wood. The whole environment seems bare after the Haller Sobieralskis' house in which every corner was crammed with vases, bowls, and decorations, and there were soft surfaces and warm dark colours. I prefer the Themersons' maisonette which is more like my father's white cupboard: spare, spartan, and utilitarian.

The house is full of paper, books, magazines. There is a mobile made by Stefan from matchboxes which hangs from the ceiling in Franciszka's studio. There is a painted stone on the mantelpiece, lampshades made from folded tracing paper.

There are also two pigeons that knock on Stefan's study window awaiting food.

One day, soon after my arrival, I ask Stefan if he knows of a Catholic church in the vicinity. He doesn't. I find one by myself in St John's Wood, and go there full of anticipation of stumbling on a sung Mass, on a Latin ritual that would re-invoke the emotions I felt so many times at a mass in Poland. The church is empty and dark. I stay around for a while, look at the holy images that now appear tawdry, recite a few Latin prayers and leave, leave for good. My need for the ritual has evaporated. After that visit, God and the Holy Family will assume a new place in my life, as part of art's iconography.

The journey to London, number fifteen, was the last journey I counted, and after three months, I stop talking about the war. Stefan says to me that one can live either in the past or in the future, and there is no doubt about which choice is possible. And from then on it is the future that becomes my abiding interest and passion.

The Themersons might have returned to Poland or to Paris after the war but circumstances conspired to keep them in England. There are contracts with publishers, commissions for Franciszka's illustrations, new opportunities of every sort that have persuaded them to stay. In the event, that bright future falters, commissions are cancelled, promises revoked, and publishers foreclosed. But by that time the decision to stay has been made, and on top of that comes my arrival. My mother's plan for my future, that I should live abroad with Franciszka and Stefan, is realised—albeit in different circumstances and a different city.

Franciszka and Stefan set about my rehabilitation. I am given English lessons by Lusia Krakowska, piano lessons by Jan Śliwiński. My faltering attempts at writing poetry are praised. I am taken to exhibitions, cinema, ballet, theatre, and skating at the Queensway Ice Rink. Franciszka gives me one of her easels

to paint on. Stefan makes me a chess set. I meet their friends—
mostly artists and writers. London just after World War II is still
the centre of Polish intellectual life. The artist Janina Konarska,
wife of Antoni Słonimski, poet, editor of *Nowa Polska*, later to
be the first President of UNESCO, makes a portrait of the three
of us: Franciszka, Stefan, and me. I am big and yellow and look
like a lioness. Janka says she is pleased that someone is there to
look after the Themersons.

I have bad teeth and so I am taken care of by a dentist; as I am
too short for my age Dr Kryszek is trying to find an appropriate
cure—I am given new insoles for my flat feet and rose hip syrup
to provide vitamin C, and I am on the way to a full recovery.

When time comes to find a school, we visit Bryanston and
King Alfred's. In the end, Franciszka and Stefan come to the

conclusion that they cannot provide me with an adequate environment at home and conclude that a boarding school would be the best solution.

They decide that Dartington would be the ideal place for me if by some miracle I were to be accepted at such short notice and with a grant. The school is liberal, co-educational, and international. There are no uniforms, and there is an emphasis on individual development. Franka writes to W. B. Curry, the headmaster of Dartington Hall School.

Franciszka's letter to W.B. Curry at Dartington:

On 4 April 1946,

Dear Sir,

I would like to place my little niece as a boarder in your School. She is of Polish nationality, twelve years old. May I ask you for the favour of accepting her after the Easter holidays. I do hope you will be able to do it.

I must apologise for applying so late, but the case is exceptional as she came to this country only two months ago. She has been in Warsaw all through the war and lost her parents in 1942. Her father was an architect, and her mother a pianist. The girl herself is quite musical and shows a lot of interest in the arts. I am an artist painter myself, and I brought her here as her nearest and only relative.

All through the war she attended schools in Poland and was in a form up to her age. She has learned a little English since she came over and can make herself understood in everyday language. As I think the best and only way to learn English is to be among English children of her age, I am very anxious to place her in a school as soon as possible. I will be most grateful if you could help me in this matter and accept her at the beginning of next term.

May I ask you at the same time to send me all the details about fees, regulations &c.

Awaiting your kind reply,
   I am yours faithfully,
Franciszka Themerson

Curry visits the Themersons in my absence. I am accepted and given a scholarship sight unseen. Franka cannot believe her luck. She feels sure that Dartington will be an ideal school for me.

I don't want to go to Dartington or to any other boarding school, but my objections are overruled. I am regaled with stories about all the different musical instruments I will be able to play, but this is hardly reassuring. I don't want to play a trumpet or anything else! I want to read and listen to the radio (which we don't have), and I don't want to go anywhere. I want to go to the cinema.

There is a farm, so there will be some animals. I capitulate. Preparations are made to equip me for the summer term, even though we are still unsure if there will be a place for me. I make some dirndl skirts. Our great friend Maga Potworowska makes me two dresses. I have pencils, pens, drawing material, some British Museum postcards to pin on my walls. I am accepted with five days' notice because one of the other pupils is not returning to school. The school train leaves Paddington station at 10.40

the following Wednesday. Franciszka and I are at Paddington in time. I get into a compartment reserved for the school pupils. I wave good-bye and carefully look at my smiling colleagues. Everybody says 'hello' and tries to engage me in conversation. I remember nothing of the long journey to Totnes. The drive to school is through beautiful countryside—very different to the familiar Polish landscape around Warsaw full of birch trees and maples. I am impressed by the sweep of the drive into Foxhole, the white building, the tennis courts.

Entrace to Foxhole

Everyone is enormously kind and helpful even though I can barely string together a sentence in English. I am provided with an interpreter, Emil Spira, the Polish piano teacher. He meets me at the entrance to Foxhole and takes me immediately to meet my new housemother. On the first floor of the 'green house' I enter a large bright room with loose covered armchairs, hand-made rugs on the floor, and pictures on the walls. At the other end, under the window, stands Bridget Edwards extending her hand to me. I rush to shake it, slide on a rug right across the room and end up on the floor at her feet. 'Welcome to Foxhole', she says helping me up.

And so starts the first chapter of my English life.

AND THEN . . .

I am shown round the school by a pupil, Janet Foyster: the dining hall, the library, gym, secretary's office, music rooms, assembly hall, the place with the daily newspapers and magazines. Then I am taken to my room on the first floor. It has a cupboard with a basin, a wardrobe with shelves, a desk, a chair, and a bed covered with a blue blanket. The window faces the school quadrangle. It will do.

A few scenes from my early life at Dartington:

I try several musical instruments, cello, clarinet, piano, only to admit that apart from the piano, I am no good at all. I join the choir. I have English lessons every day and initially I go to classes in geography and mathematics, French and Latin. I learn to play hockey and tennis and to ride a bike, which the Themersons send me from London. When it comes to swimming lessons, before the first lesson, I hide in the lavatory, knowing that the children swim naked in the open air swimming pool and I cannot cope with that. My tutor, Jack Hamshere, finds me, knocks on the door and explains that anybody who wants to wear a swimming costume can do so. I grab the woollen 1920s style yellow swimming costume which Franciszka gave me and follow Jack to the pool. There are lots of children, all naked, with one exception. I want to be, I must be like everybody else, my yellow swimming costume would be very noticeable, and so I strip in five seconds and rush into the pool for my first lesson in dog paddle. There are many first steps. On another day, 'Can you ride a horse?' asks the teacher as a group of us is waiting to go riding, 'Yes, of course', I say. I am put on a horse and fall off at once. Lessons follow.

By the end of the summer term I can swim, ride a bike, and speak English. My time at Dartington is not without problems, mistakes, and adjustments, social, emotional, and academic, but the journey gets easier.

When, three years later, Franciszka receives my School Certificate results, with Jack Hamshere's congratulations and a suitable number of credits, she bursts into tears. I am a normal child after all.

For five years Dartington Hall School is my second home. It leads me to the next stage of my life. Apart from schoolwork I develop a passion for the theatre, join the entertainments committee, and produce a cabaret for school half-term parties. I also work in the Barn Theatre of Dartington Hall. I know what I want to do, I want to direct plays, cabaret, I want to produce witty, intellectual entertainments. Well, that's my ambition. And so, after taking more exams and leaving Dartington in the summer of 1951, I go to the Old Vic Theatre School directed by Michel Saint-Denis, Glen Byam Shaw, and George Devine, in West Dulwich, for the Production Course. Due to lack of funds, the school closes after one year. My course is curtailed. There follow several jobs in the theatre, as stage manager and stage director, and then a succession of mundane jobs which introduce me, at the time much to my dismay, to various aspects of office work, ending with assistant editorship of the *British Welding Journal*.

Meanwhile, the Themersons, apart from their personal work, Franciszka in painting and Stefan in writing, continue to run Gaberbocchus Press, which they founded in 1948.

In 1957, below the offices of the press, in the basement of 42a Formosa Street in Maida Vale, they launch the Gaberbocchus Common Room, a meeting place for people interested in art and science. During the next two years, there are film screenings, lectures, play readings, recitals, and discussion. It is there that I come across ideas that a few years later will be referred to as Pop Art; where I learn about cybernetics; and where I marry my interest in avant-garde art to an interest in science and technology.

An evening at Gaberbocchus Common Room

By 1958 I no longer want to work for the *British Welding Journal*. I buy *Writers' and Artists' Yearbook* and start with the letter A, applying for jobs. My tenth letter goes to *Art News & Review*. Dr Richard Gainsborough rings me up. 'We are looking for a secretary', 'I am not a secretary', I say, 'I am an assistant editor'. 'What can you do?' 'I can edit, proofread, do layout, type, do accounts up to trial balance, operate a switchboard'. 'Bring a sample article'. I write an article about Richard Smith, take it along and get the job. 'How many reviews can you write per issue?', 'How many do you want me to write?'. 'Seven', says Dr G. For the following two years I write as many reviews as I can. I have seven pseudonyms. My best articles are written under the name Clifford N. Wright, and then, in order of importance, Jasia Reichardt, Janet Ceglo, Melousine Alexander, Mark Sebastian, Anton Brodnik, and Orlando Kokoschka. In 1959, Dr Gainsborough is absent for several months due to illness. I run the paper, make it more avant-garde, change its style a bit.

When Dr G., as he is called, returns to the office, he finds a large pile of correspondence on my desk and practically nothing on his. He gives me the sack with two weeks' notice. While I am still employed I hurry to join AICA and the National Union of Journalists.

•

And now, briefly, the rest. With 1960 begins the first period of my freelance life. I start writing for *Apollo, Architectural Design, Art d'Aujourd'hui, Metro*, and other journals. My freelance work develops. I am never paid adequately, often not at all, but the important thing is to work. I organise exhibitions, give talks, sit on juries, and eventually get my next job in 1963 at the Institute of Contemporary Arts as assistant director. Because the organisation is open to new ideas and experiment it is possible to organise various exhibitions that had not been seen in London before, among them 'Between Poetry and Painting', an exhibition of concrete poetry; 'Cybernetic Serendipity', the computer and the arts; 'Fluorescent Chrysanthemum', Japanese design, animation, and music; and 'Play Orbit', an exhibition of toys by artists.

I leave the ICA in 1971, teach at the Architectural Association, write for the *New Scientist*, broadcast, give lectures. From 1974 until 1976, I work as director of the Whitechapel Art Gallery, and that is my last proper job. My concern with the borderlines of art remains an abiding passion. I continue to write, publish a book on robots, teach, and spend some time working in Japan. After Franciszka and Stefan Themerson die in 1988, I organise the Themerson Archive in collaboration with Nick Wadley and with help from many others (who are all acknowledged in the eight-volume catalogue of the archive, completed in 2010). This archive is very much a counterpart to my story, not only because I was brought up by the Themersons but also because I was involved in their creative and intellectual life and in the world of Gaberbocchus Press.

Living with the Themersons for ten years I become used to meeting artists, philosophers, writers, translators, scientists, all in a milieu where work and ideas are of primary importance. That too very gradually becomes my modus vivendi. Work is more important than cooking, and this should not surprise any-one who read *Mr Rouse Builds His House*, a book for children written by Stefan in 1938, about the problems and triumphs of building a house, which in the end has no kitchen. As a child I had not noticed this gap.

After arriving in London, on the 28th of January 1946, I barely notice that life is so spare, with bare surfaces, penetrat-ing cold, rationing, pea-soup fogs, and the gas or electric-ity cut off when the bills can't be paid. There is still more of everything than I am used to, certainly a lot more books, and the Themersons' friends find clothes for me to wear. Franciszka and Stefan are busy working and I, meanwhile, look for excitement—provided during my first few months in London by the Science Museum, and then, until I learn enough English, by walking around town whenever I can find anyone speaking Polish to accompany me.

•

Why do the Themersons start a publishing company? After making their two shorts for the Polish Film Unit—*Calling Mr Smith*, an antiwar film, and *The Eye and the Ear*, about the visualisation of sound—funding for film all but disappeared. As the Themersons wrote, illustrated, designed, and published books in Poland during the 1930s, publishing seems an opportunity to start something through which they can again engage the world. Gaberbocchus Press is launched in 1948. Some fifty years later it would be called (by the Victoria and Albert Museum) 'the first avant-garde publishing house in England'. By the time Gaberbocchus is transferred to Amsterdam in 1979, there would be sixty titles in its catalogue, including the first English translations of Alfred Jarry, Raymond Queneau, Kurt Schwitters, Raoul Hausmann, Anatol Stern, Henri Chopin, Pol-Dives, J. H. Sainmont, and Christian Dietrich Grabbe; there would be poems by Stevie Smith, illustrated by the author, and then Bertrand Russell's take on human behaviour in *The Good Citizen's Alphabet*, illustrated, like many of the other books, by Franciszka. There would be pochoirs of the river Thames by Gwen Barnard, detective

150

stories by Oswell Blakeston, memoirs by George Buchanan, poems by Patrick Fetherston, Hugo Manning, James Laughlin, and David Miller. Cozette de Charmoy would present a pictorial novel, and Harold Lang and Kenneth Tynan would write a play for radio. Stefan would publish twenty books of his own, including novels, philosophy, semantic poetry, and an opera. Franciszka would publish two books of drawings.

Until Gaberbocchus moves to Formosa Street in 1957, by which time I will have left home, its office is next to my room. This is where books are packed and invoices written. Preparation for printing, design, layout, and photography is done by Franciszka in her study upstairs on a large trestle table, on which we can also play ping-pong. I help very occasionally folding book jackets, collating pages, sticking down press cuttings. But I am getting busy with my own life, and soon work of any sort at home gets in the way of my spending time with friends and going to jazz clubs. My teenage years are similar to those of most young people who can avoid having responsibilities thrust upon them. Franciszka and Stefan don't interfere, and there is only one rule: boyfriends must be invited home.

I reach my twenties before I can properly appreciate what the Themersons do, before I have some measure of the significance of their work, and before I can see them objectively. It also takes years for my wartime scars to stop interfering with my life, for me to accept the world around me and at the same time to give it a shape I can live with.

●

In 1996 Maria Elena de la Iglesia publishes a book of staff memories of the early years of Dartington Hall School. In it, one of the housemothers writes about a girl whose parents died in the camps and who was hysterical and cried and wanted to be mothered. By then probably nobody would have guessed that I was the person that Bea Hamshere referred to.

WHO'S WHO

LISTED BY FIRST LETTER OF FIRST NAME
THOSE WHO SURVIVED THE WAR ARE INDENTED

Anka Poznańska, a cousin, very close to Stefan and his family. She called Stefan 'Kotulek' and signed her letters to him 'Kotulkowa Anka', which suggests that she was close to him when he was very young.

Cecylia (Cesia) Chajkin, my paternal grandmother. Sewek's mother. The family moved from Łódź to Warsaw. She lived at ulica Dzielna, then after a few years moved with Michał and Paweł to ulica Nowogrodzka, on the corner of ulica Marszałkowska. Michał had his office there.

Franciszka (Franka/Franeczka) Themerson (1907–1988), my aunt. Daughter of Łucja and Jakub Weinles, wife of Stefan Themerson, sister of Maryla Chaykin. Studied art and the piano. Painter, filmmaker, illustrator. Zdzisław Libera remembered her playing the piano. When the war broke out, she and her husband, Stefan Themerson, were living in Paris. In September 1939, she volunteered for service with the Polish forces and worked as cartographer for the Polish government-in-exile in Paris, then Lourdes, and later in

Angers. In June 1940 the entire operation moved to London and that is where Franciszka continued her work. Stefan joined her in the summer of 1942 and they continued to live in London for the rest of their lives.

Halina Pągowska, architect. Colleague of Seweryn Chaykin. She rescued me in 1942. She changed her surname to Czyżyńska and continued to live in Warsaw.

Hania Kawa, cousin of the Themersons. Lived in Bucharest and acted as a post office sending and copying messages and letters to members of the family. She visited London after the war.

Heniek (Henryk) Haller Sobieralski, husband of Ludka, father of Wandzia and Jaś. Owned a timber store; appeared in the Themersons' film *The Adventure of a Good Citizen*. Shared Maryla's flat in the Warsaw ghetto. Collected me from the nuns in Pustelnik in 1945. The name 'Sobieralski' was a wartime acquisition from the documents of one of Jaś's friends who died. After the war he was the mayor of Sierpc, a small town northwest of Warsaw.

Herman Chajkin, my grandfather, whom I never met. Father of Stach, Sewek, Michał, and Paweł, husband of Cecylia [Cesia] Zając, sister of Zdzisław Libera's mother. Violinist, studied with Stanisław Barcewicz. During the latter part of his life he ran a printing/publishing business producing invitation cards and visiting cards to be sold in stationery shops.

Jakub Weinles (d. 1938), my maternal grandfather. Father of Maryla and Franciszka, husband of Łucja Kaufman. Painter in the traditional style. His studio was burnt down on the first day of the war and most of his oeuvre was destroyed.

Jasia (Janka), that's me. Daughter of Maryla and Seweryn Chaykin.

Jerzy Michałowski, Seweryn Chaykin's colleague, friend of the Themersons, Ambassador to the court of St James's twice, Ambassador in Washington, and to the United Nations. His second wife and the mother of his sons, Peter and Stefan, was Mira Złotowska.

Łucja Weinles, née Kaufman (d. 1942), my maternal grandmother. Wife of the painter Jakub Weinles, mother of Maryla and Franciszka, sister of Władek Kaufman and the painter, Leon Kamir. Pianist. She committed suicide with other members of the family at Zofiówka in Otwock in the summer of 1942.

Ludka (Ludwika) Haller Sobieralska, wife of Heniek, mother of Wandzia, was related to both Franciszka and Stefan. She found me in 1945 and advised Franciszka in London. I lived with her and her family between November 1945 and January 1946, prior to coming to London.

Maria Tywonek, a helpful Aryan woman who probably worked for members of the Chajkin family. She posted the letters from Maryla and Łucja to Franciszka outside the ghetto.

Maryla Chaykin, née Weinles (1900–1942), my mother. Wife of Seweryn (Sewek) Chaykin, sister of Franciszka Themerson. Pianist and illustrator. She completed her studies at the conservatorium in the class of Henry Melcer, then studied at the Warsaw Academy of Fine Art. I was together with her in the Warsaw ghetto until I left in the summer of 1942. She stayed together with Sewek and died in Treblinka.

Michał Chajkin, my uncle. Younger brother of Sewek, husband of (Halina?) Berman. Lawyer. Michał with his wife were also in the Warsaw ghetto but moved to the Aryan side in January 1943. They both died in Auschwitz.

Mira and Ignacy, Złotowski, friends of the Themersons from Paris. He was a scientist, she was a writer, journalist, and translator, later the wife of Jerzy Michałowski. Mira and Ignacy succeeded in getting to America in 1940, where they separated. She and Jerzy Michałowski, Polish Ambassador to the Court of St James's, arrived in London in 1946.

Paweł Chajkin, my uncle. Sewek's younger brother. Lawyer. Survived the war in Russia, joined General Anders, spent some time in Persia, fought in Monte Cassino, and in 1947 arrived in England and settled there. Married Mira Piechocka and had two children, my cousins, Anna and Michael.

Seweryn Chaykin (1898–1942), my father. Son of Cecylia Chajkin, Maryla's husband, brother of Stach, Michał, and Paweł.

He changed his surname from Chajkin to Chaykin. Engineer/architect. Before the war, he worked on social housing in Warsaw. During the war, before joining his family in the Warsaw ghetto in October 1941, he was in Lwów and later in Kraków, but I have no information about his movements at that time. Died in Treblinka.

Stach (Stanisław) Chajkin, my uncle. Older brother of Sewek, husband of Daria Lifszyc (Dasza), separated after a few years, father of Wisia [Ludwika]. Chemist who played the cello, was involved with Polish Independence in Polska Organizacja Wojskowa, POW, received Cross of Independence. With his mother and Wisia, he shared the flat with my mother and grandmother and the Haller Sobieralskis in the Warsaw ghetto.

Stefan (Stefek/Kotulek) Themerson (1910–1988), my uncle. Son of Dr Mieczysław Themerson, husband of Franciszka, brother of Dr Irena (Irka/Irenka) Miller. Writer, poet, filmmaker, publisher. Together with Franciszka, he moved to Paris in 1938. At the outbreak of the war, he volunteered to join the Polish army. At the end of May, Stefan's regiment was marching through Brittany but within two or three weeks, it was disbanded, 'Sauve qui peut!' Stefan walked to occupied Paris and eventually found his way to a Polish Red Cross Hostel in Voiron. He stayed there until the summer of 1942, when after almost endless complications, he was able to join Franciszka in London.

Stefanja Zahorska, film critic, friend of the Themersons

from Warsaw. After the war, she was in Paris and in London, and was in touch with the Themersons.

Teresa Żarnower, artist, good friend of the Themersons. She was in France in 1940, in Angers with Franciszka. She made it to Lisbon and then New York. She helped the Themersons in every way possible but mainly by forwarding mail and, while she was in Lisbon, sending parcels to Franciszka's family in Warsaw.

Wandzia (Wanda) Haller Sobieralska (7 June 1920–20 April 2009), my cousin. Daughter of Ludka and Heniek, wife of Genek Wilczyński. Accountant. Lived in Warsaw.

Wisia Chajkin, my first cousin. Stach's daughter.

Zdzisław Libin (Libera), my cousin. Sewek's first cousin, son of Cecylia's sister, younger brother of Antoni Libin. They also lived on ulica Śliska in the ghetto, on the other side of the street, probably number 62. During the evacuation of the ghetto, Cecylia moved in with Zdzisław and Antoni and their mother. The two sisters were taken away on 6th August 1942. Zdzisław at the time was employed in a workshop producing things for the Germans, on ulica Nowolipki. He saw Stach after 6th August. During his stay in the ghetto he taught in underground schools, among them in Gimnazjum Spójnia. He described it in an article 'Szkolnictwo w dzielnicy zamkniętej', in a book entitled *Niezwyciężona szkoła* (Indomitable School). He spent a holiday in 1926 in Falenica with the Weinleses and he remembers Łucja playing an arabesque by Debussy on the piano. After the war, he too tried to find me. He and his wife Helena had one son, Antoni, writer and expert on Beckett. They lived in Warsaw.

CALENDARIUM

1 September 1939
Outbreak of World War II.

28 September 1939
Surrender of Warsaw.

28 October 1939
The Germans order a census of the Jewish population in Warsaw.

23 November 1939
Order for Jews to wear armbands with the Star of David.

1 April 1940
Beginning of the construction of a wall around the ghetto, referred to by the Nazis as 'the area threatened by the outbreak of disease'.

14 June 1940
The Germans march into Paris.

19 June 1940

The Polish government-in-exile is moved to London.

24 August 1940

Beginning of the London Blitz.

13–21 October 1940

Heavy raids on London.

16 November 1940

The ghetto is closed. The area is surrounded by a three-metre-high wall. More than 400,000 people live in 1483 houses. Food deliveries are stopped.

January–March 1941

Resettlement to the ghetto of Jews living in the Warsaw district.

19 March 1941

German raids on London resume.

July 1941

The term 'Final Solution' begins to be used.
A Jew is defined by the Nuremberg Laws of 1935 as any person with one Jewish grandparent.

15 October 1941

Death penalty for Jews who leave the ghetto without authorisation.

26 April 1942

Construction of a wooden bridge above ulica Chłodna to link the 'small' and the 'big' ghettos.

22 July 1942

Beginning of the 'Great Deportation Action' (Grossaktion Warsaw). Every day from Umschlagplatz, people are sent to one of the extermination camps, generally Treblinka. Before the end of the Action some 300,000 people have been deported.

19 August 1942

Liquidation of Zofiówka (Otwock).

10 October 1942

Liquidation of the 'small ghetto'.

21 September 1942

The end of the Great Deportation. Creation of a residual ghetto.

15 November 1942

A report for the Polish government-in-exile in London and the Allies is prepared in the ghetto, based on the material of the secret archive of E. Ringelblum.

18–21 January 1943

New deportation campaign meets with resistance.

19 April 1943

SS troops enter the ghetto.

The Warsaw Ghetto Uprising begins.

20 April 1943

Massacre in the Warsaw ghetto.

12 May 1943

Szmul Zygielbojm, in London, writes a letter to the President of the Republic of Poland and commits suicide as a protest against the inaction 'in which the world watches and permits the destruction of the Jewish people'.

16 May 1943

SS General Jürgen Stroop reports '. . . the Jewish quarter is no more'.

3 September 1943

Murder of the last Warsaw Jews in Majdanek, Trawniki, and Treblinka.

17 January 1945

Liberation of Warsaw by the Russians.

8 May 1945

V-E Day.

THANK YOU

to friends who took interest, aided and abetted, corrected mistakes, advised, encouraged, and believed the project to be worthwhile.

This book would never have been started without the persuasive advice of Hidé Ishiguro, nor completed without the involvement of Nick Wadley, who held my hand while I dithered among these memories, scanned pictures, and helped to make sense of this story. Nick designed front cover with my photo and back cover based on various children's drawings by Franciszka Themerson.

The pictures of *Żywe literki* on page 15 were scanned from the 1928 book by the National Public Library of Warsaw.

The photograph of Foxhole on page 151 comes from the Royal Institute of British Architects.

Photographs of the Themersons and the watercolour by Janina Konarska are in the Themerson Archive.

I am also grateful to John O'Brien of Dalkey Archive Press for taking this book under his wing, to Jeremy M. Davies for his sensitive editing, and to Aida Giurgianu for her meticulous work on the design.

JASIA REICHARDT is a writer on art and exhibition organiser. She was born in Poland, educated in England, and has lived in London most of her life. She was Assistant Director of the ICA in London, 1963–71, and Director of the Whitechapel Art Gallery, 1974–76. She has written several books on art's connections with other disciplines and contributed to many journals worldwide. She has taught at the Architectural Association and other colleges. Since 1990, with Nick Wadley, she has organised and catalogued the Themerson Archive.

PETROS ABATZOGLOU, *What Does Mrs. Freeman Want?*
MICHAL AJVAZ, *The Golden Age.*
The Other City.
PIERRE ALBERT-BIROT, *Grabinoulor.*
YUZ ALESHKOVSKY, *Kangaroo.*
FELIPE ALFAU, *Chromos.*
Locos.
JOÃO ALMINO, *The Book of Emotions.*
IVAN ÂNGELO, *The Celebration.*
The Tower of Glass.
DAVID ANTIN, *Talking.*
ANTÓNIO LOBO ANTUNES, *Knowledge of Hell.*
The Splendor of Portugal.
ALAIN ARIAS-MISSON, *Theatre of Incest.*
IFTIKHAR ARIF AND WAQAS KHWAJA, EDS., *Modern Poetry of Pakistan.*
JOHN ASHBERY AND JAMES SCHUYLER, *A Nest of Ninnies.*
ROBERT ASHLEY, *Perfect Lives.*
GABRIELA AVIGUR-ROTEM, *Heatwave and Crazy Birds.*
HEIMRAD BÄCKER, *transcript.*
DJUNA BARNES, *Ladies Almanack.*
Ryder.
JOHN BARTH, *LETTERS.*
Sabbatical.
DONALD BARTHELME, *The King.*
Paradise.
SVETISLAV BASARA, *Chinese Letter.*
MIQUEL BAUÇÀ, *The Siege in the Room.*
RENÉ BELLETTO, *Dying.*
MAREK BIEŃCZYK, *Transparency.*
MARK BINELLI, *Sacco and Vanzetti Must Die!*
ANDREI BITOV, *Pushkin House.*
ANDREJ BLATNIK, *You Do Understand.*
LOUIS PAUL BOON, *Chapel Road.*
My Little War.
Summer in Termuren.
ROGER BOYLAN, *Killoyle.*
IGNÁCIO DE LOYOLA BRANDÃO, *Anonymous Celebrity.*
The Good-Bye Angel.
Teeth under the Sun.
Zero.
BONNIE BREMSER, *Troia: Mexican Memoirs.*
CHRISTINE BROOKE-ROSE, *Amalgamemnon.*
BRIGID BROPHY, *In Transit.*
MEREDITH BROSNAN, *Mr. Dynamite.*
GERALD L. BRUNS, *Modern Poetry and the Idea of Language.*
EVGENY BUNIMOVICH AND J. KATES, EDS., *Contemporary Russian Poetry: An Anthology.*
GABRIELLE BURTON, *Heartbreak Hotel.*
MICHEL BUTOR, *Degrees.*
Mobile.
Portrait of the Artist as a Young Ape.
G. CABRERA INFANTE, *Infante's Inferno.*
Three Trapped Tigers.
JULIETA CAMPOS, *The Fear of Losing Eurydice.*
ANNE CARSON, *Eros the Bittersweet.*
ORLY CASTEL-BLOOM, *Dolly City.*
CAMILO JOSÉ CELA, *Christ versus Arizona.*
The Family of Pascual Duarte.
The Hive.
LOUIS-FERDINAND CÉLINE, *Castle to Castle.*
Conversations with Professor Y.
London Bridge.

Normance.
North.
Rigadoon.
MARIE CHAIX, *The Laurels of Lake Constance.*
HUGO CHARTERIS, *The Tide Is Right.*
JEROME CHARYN, *The Tar Baby.*
ERIC CHEVILLARD, *Demolishing Nisard.*
LUIS CHITARRONI, *The No Variations.*
MARC CHOLODENKO, *Mordechai Schamz.*
JOSHUA COHEN, *Witz.*
EMILY HOLMES COLEMAN, *The Shutter of Snow.*
ROBERT COOVER, *A Night at the Movies.*
STANLEY CRAWFORD, *Log of the S.S. The Mrs Unguentine.*
Some Instructions to My Wife.
ROBERT CREELEY, *Collected Prose.*
RENÉ CREVEL, *Putting My Foot in It.*
RALPH CUSACK, *Cadenza.*
SUSAN DAITCH, *L.C.*
Storytown.
NICHOLAS DELBANCO, *The Count of Concord.*
Sherbrookes.
NIGEL DENNIS, *Cards of Identity.*
PETER DIMOCK, *A Short Rhetoric for Leaving the Family.*
ARIEL DORFMAN, *Konfidenz.*
COLEMAN DOWELL,
The Houses of Children.
Island People.
Too Much Flesh and Jabez.
ARKADII DRAGOMOSHCHENKO, *Dust.*
RIKKI DUCORNET, *The Complete Butcher's Tales.*
The Fountains of Neptune.
The Jade Cabinet.
The One Marvelous Thing.
Phosphor in Dreamland.
The Stain.
The Word "Desire."
WILLIAM EASTLAKE, *The Bamboo Bed.*
Castle Keep.
Lyric of the Circle Heart.
JEAN ECHENOZ, *Chopin's Move.*
STANLEY ELKIN, *A Bad Man.*
Boswell: A Modern Comedy.
Criers and Kibitzers, Kibitzers and Criers.
The Dick Gibson Show.
The Franchiser.
George Mills.
The Living End.
The MacGuffin.
The Magic Kingdom.
Mrs. Ted Bliss.
The Rabbi of Lud.
Van Gogh's Room at Arles.
FRANÇOIS EMMANUEL, *Invitation to a Voyage.*
ANNIE ERNAUX, *Cleaned Out.*
SALVADOR ESPRIU, *Ariadne in the Grotesque Labyrinth.*
LAUREN FAIRBANKS, *Muzzle Thyself.*
Sister Carrie.
LESLIE A. FIEDLER, *Love and Death in the American Novel.*
JUAN FILLOY, *Faction.*
Op Oloop.
ANDY FITCH, *Pop Poetics.*
GUSTAVE FLAUBERT, *Bouvard and Pécuchet.*
KASS FLEISHER, *Talking out of School.*

FORD MADOX FORD,
The March of Literature.
JON FOSSE, *Aliss at the Fire.*
Melancholy.
MAX FRISCH, *I'm Not Stiller.*
Man in the Holocene.
CARLOS FUENTES, *Christopher Unborn.*
Distant Relations.
Terra Nostra.
Vlad.
Where the Air Is Clear.
TAKEHIKO FUKUNAGA, *Flowers of Grass.*
WILLIAM GADDIS, *J R.*
The Recognitions.
JANICE GALLOWAY, *Foreign Parts.*
The Trick Is to Keep Breathing.
WILLIAM H. GASS, *Cartesian Sonata*
and Other Novellas.
Finding a Form.
A Temple of Texts.
The Tunnel.
Willie Masters' Lonesome Wife.
GÉRARD GAVARRY, *Hoppla! 1 2 3.*
Making a Novel.
ETIENNE GILSON,
The Arts of the Beautiful.
Forms and Substances in the Arts.
C. S. GISCOMBE, *Giscome Road.*
Here.
Prairie Style.
DOUGLAS GLOVER, *Bad News of the Heart.*
The Enamoured Knight.
WITOLD GOMBROWICZ,
A Kind of Testament.
PAULO EMÍLIO SALES GOMES, *P's Three*
Women.
KAREN ELIZABETH GORDON, *The Red Shoes.*
GEORGI GOSPODINOV, *Natural Novel.*
JUAN GOYTISOLO, *Count Julian.*
Exiled from Almost Everywhere.
Juan the Landless.
Makbara.
Marks of Identity.
PATRICK GRAINVILLE, *The Cave of Heaven.*
HENRY GREEN, *Back.*
Blindness.
Concluding.
Doting.
Nothing.
JACK GREEN, *Fire the Bastards!*
JIŘÍ GRUŠA, *The Questionnaire.*
GABRIEL GUDDING,
Rhode Island Notebook.
MELA HARTWIG, *Am I a Redundant*
Human Being?
JOHN HAWKES, *The Passion Artist.*
Whistlejacket.
ELIZABETH HEIGHWAY, ED., *Contemporary*
Georgian Fiction.
ALEKSANDAR HEMON, ED.,
Best European Fiction.
AIDAN HIGGINS, *Balcony of Europe.*
A Bestiary.
Blind Man's Bluff.
Bornholm Night-Ferry.
Darkling Plain: Texts for the Air.
Flotsam and Jetsam.
Langrishe, Go Down.
Scenes from a Receding Past.
Windy Arbours.
KEIZO HINO, *Isle of Dreams.*
KAZUSHI HOSAKA, *Plainsong.*

ALDOUS HUXLEY, *Antic Hay.*
Crome Yellow.
Point Counter Point.
Those Barren Leaves.
Time Must Have a Stop.
NAOYUKI II, *The Shadow of a Blue Cat.*
MIKHAIL IOSSEL AND JEFF PARKER, EDS.,
Amerika: Russian Writers View the
United States.
DRAGO JANČAR, *The Galley Slave.*
GERT JONKE, *The Distant Sound.*
Geometric Regional Novel.
Homage to Czerny.
The System of Vienna.
JACQUES JOUET, *Mountain R.*
Savage.
Upstaged.
CHARLES JULIET, *Conversations with*
Samuel Beckett and Bram van
Velde.
MIEKO KANAI, *The Word Book.*
YORAM KANIUK, *Life on Sandpaper.*
HUGH KENNER, *The Counterfeiters.*
Flaubert, Joyce and Beckett:
The Stoic Comedians.
Joyce's Voices.
DANILO KIŠ, *The Attic.*
Garden, Ashes.
The Lute and the Scars
Psalm 44.
A Tomb for Boris Davidovich.
ANITA KONKKA, *A Fool's Paradise.*
GEORGE KONRÁD, *The City Builder.*
TADEUSZ KONWICKI, *A Minor Apocalypse.*
The Polish Complex.
MENIS KOUMANDAREAS, *Koula.*
ELAINE KRAF, *The Princess of 72nd Street.*
JIM KRUSOE, *Iceland.*
AYŞE KULIN, *Farewell: A Mansion in*
Occupied Istanbul.
EWA KURYLUK, *Century 21.*
EMILIO LASCANO TEGUI, *On Elegance*
While Sleeping.
ERIC LAURRENT, *Do Not Touch.*
HERVÉ LE TELLIER, *The Sextine Chapel.*
A Thousand Pearls (for a Thousand
Pennies)
VIOLETTE LEDUC, *La Bâtarde.*
EDOUARD LEVÉ, *Autoportrait.*
Suicide.
MARIO LEVI, *Istanbul Was a Fairy Tale.*
SUZANNE JILL LEVINE, *The Subversive*
Scribe: Translating Latin
American Fiction.
DEBORAH LEVY, *Billy and Girl.*
Pillow Talk in Europe and Other
Places.
JOSÉ LEZAMA LIMA, *Paradiso.*
ROSA LIKSOM, *Dark Paradise.*
OSMAN LINS, *Avalovara.*
The Queen of the Prisons of Greece.
ALF MAC LOCHLAINN,
The Corpus in the Library.
Out of Focus.
RON LOEWINSOHN, *Magnetic Field(s).*
MINA LOY, *Stories and Essays of Mina Loy.*
BRIAN LYNCH, *The Winner of Sorrow.*
D. KEITH MANO, *Take Five.*
MICHELINE AHARONIAN MARCOM,
The Mirror in the Well.
BEN MARCUS,
The Age of Wire and String.

SELECTED DALKEY ARCHIVE TITLES

WALLACE MARKFIELD,
  Teitlebaum's Window.
  To an Early Grave.
DAVID MARKSON, Reader's Block.
  Springer's Progress.
  Wittgenstein's Mistress.
CAROLE MASO, AVA.
LADISLAV MATEJKA AND KRYSTYNA
  POMORSKA, EDS.,
  Readings in Russian Poetics:
    Formalist and Structuralist Views.
HARRY MATHEWS,
  The Case of the Persevering Maltese:
    Collected Essays.
  Cigarettes.
  The Conversions.
  The Human Country: New and
    Collected Stories.
  The Journalist.
  My Life in CIA.
  Singular Pleasures.
  The Sinking of the Odradek
    Stadium.
  Tlooth.
  20 Lines a Day.
JOSEPH MCELROY,
  Night Soul and Other Stories.
THOMAS MCGONIGLE,
  Going to Patchogue.
ROBERT L. MCLAUGHLIN, ED., Innovations:
  An Anthology of Modern &
    Contemporary Fiction.
ABDELWAHAB MEDDEB, Talismano.
GERHARD MEIER, Isle of the Dead.
HERMAN MELVILLE, The Confidence-Man.
AMANDA MICHALOPOULOU, I'd Like.
STEVEN MILLHAUSER, The Barnum Museum.
  In the Penny Arcade.
RALPH J. MILLS, JR., Essays on Poetry.
MOMUS, The Book of Jokes.
CHRISTINE MONTALBETTI, The Origin of Man.
  Western.
OLIVE MOORE, Spleen.
NICHOLAS MOSLEY, Accident.
  Assassins.
  Catastrophe Practice.
  Children of Darkness and Light.
  Experience and Religion.
  A Garden of Trees.
  God's Hazard.
  The Hesperides Tree.
  Hopeful Monsters.
  Imago Bird.
  Impossible Object.
  Inventing God.
  Judith.
  Look at the Dark.
  Natalie Natalia.
  Paradoxes of Peace.
  Serpent.
  Time at War.
  The Uses of Slime Mould:
    Essays of Four Decades.
WARREN MOTTE,
  Fables of the Novel: French Fiction
    since 1990.
  Fiction Now: The French Novel in
    the 21st Century.
  Oulipo: A Primer of Potential
    Literature.
GERALD MURNANE, Barley Patch.
  Inland.

YVES NAVARRE, Our Share of Time.
  Sweet Tooth.
DOROTHY NELSON, In Night's City.
  Tar and Feathers.
ESHKOL NEVO, Homesick.
WILFRIDO D. NOLLEDO, But for the Lovers.
FLANN O'BRIEN, At Swim-Two-Birds.
  At War.
  The Best of Myles.
  The Dalkey Archive.
  Further Cuttings.
  The Hard Life.
  The Poor Mouth.
  The Third Policeman.
CLAUDE OLLIER, The Mise-en-Scène.
  Wert and the Life Without End.
GIOVANNI ORELLI, Walaschek's Dream.
PATRIK OUŘEDNÍK, Europeana.
  The Opportune Moment, 1855.
BORIS PAHOR, Necropolis.
FERNANDO DEL PASO, News from the Empire.
  Palinuro of Mexico.
ROBERT PINGET, The Inquisitory.
  Mahu or The Material.
  Trio.
A. G. PORTA, The No World Concerto.
MANUEL PUIG, Betrayed by Rita Hayworth.
  The Buenos Aires Affair.
  Heartbreak Tango.
RAYMOND QUENEAU, The Last Days.
  Odile.
  Pierrot Mon Ami.
  Saint Glinglin.
ANN QUIN, Berg.
  Passages.
  Three.
  Tripticks.
ISHMAEL REED, The Free-Lance Pallbearers.
  The Last Days of Louisiana Red.
  Ishmael Reed: The Plays.
  Juice!
  Reckless Eyeballing.
  The Terrible Threes.
  The Terrible Twos.
  Yellow Back Radio Broke-Down.
JASIA REICHARDT, 15 Journeys Warsaw
  to London.
NOËLLE REVAZ, With the Animals.
JOÃO UBALDO RIBEIRO, House of the
  Fortunate Buddhas.
JEAN RICARDOU, Place Names.
RAINER MARIA RILKE, The Notebooks of
  Malte Laurids Brigge.
JULIÁN RÍOS, The House of Ulysses.
  Larva: A Midsummer Night's Babel.
  Poundemonium.
  Procession of Shadows.
AUGUSTO ROA BASTOS, I the Supreme.
DANIËL ROBBERECHTS, Arriving in Avignon.
JEAN ROLIN, The Explosion of the
  Radiator Hose.
OLIVIER ROLIN, Hotel Crystal.
ALIX CLEO ROUBAUD, Alix's Journal.
JACQUES ROUBAUD, The Form of a
  City Changes Faster, Alas, Than
    the Human Heart.
  The Great Fire of London.
  Hortense in Exile.
  Hortense Is Abducted.
  The Loop.
  Mathematics:
  The Plurality of Worlds of Lewis.

FOR A FULL LIST OF PUBLICATIONS, VISIT:
www.dalkeyarchive.com

SELECTED DALKEY ARCHIVE TITLES

The Princess Hoppy.
Some Thing Black.
LEON S. ROUDIEZ, *French Fiction Revisited.*
RAYMOND ROUSSEL, *Impressions of Africa.*
VEDRANA RUDAN, *Night.*
STIG SÆTERBAKKEN, *Siamese.*
LYDIE SALVAYRE, *The Company of Ghosts.*
Everyday Life.
The Lecture.
Portrait of the Writer as a
Domesticated Animal.
The Power of Flies.
LUIS RAFAEL SÁNCHEZ,
Macho Camacho's Beat.
SEVERO SARDUY, *Cobra & Maitreya.*
NATHALIE SARRAUTE,
Do You Hear Them?
Martereau.
The Planetarium.
ARNO SCHMIDT, *Collected Novellas.*
Collected Stories.
Nobodaddy's Children.
Two Novels.
ASAF SCHURR, *Motti.*
CHRISTINE SCHUTT, *Nightwork.*
GAIL SCOTT, *My Paris.*
DAMION SEARLS, *What We Were Doing*
and Where We Were Going.
JUNE AKERS SEESE,
Is This What Other Women Feel Too?
What Waiting Really Means.
BERNARD SHARE, *Inish.*
Transit.
AURELIE SHEEHAN, *Jack Kerouac Is Pregnant.*
VIKTOR SHKLOVSKY, *Bowstring.*
Knight's Move.
A Sentimental Journey:
Memoirs 1917–1922.
Energy of Delusion: A Book on Plot.
Literature and Cinematography.
Theory of Prose.
Third Factory.
Zoo, or Letters Not about Love.
CLAUDE SIMON, *The Invitation.*
PIERRE SINIAC, *The Collaborators.*
KJERSTI A. SKOMSVOLD, *The Faster I Walk,*
the Smaller I Am.
JOSEF ŠKVORECKÝ, *The Engineer of*
Human Souls.
GILBERT SORRENTINO,
Aberration of Starlight.
Blue Pastoral.
Crystal Vision.
Imaginative Qualities of Actual
Things.
Mulligan Stew.
Pack of Lies.
Red the Fiend.
The Sky Changes.
Something Said.
Splendide-Hôtel.
Steelwork.
Under the Shadow.
W. M. SPACKMAN, *The Complete Fiction.*
ANDRZEJ STASIUK, *Dukla.*
Fado.
GERTRUDE STEIN, *Lucy Church Amiably.*
The Making of Americans.
A Novel of Thank You.
LARS SVENDSEN, *A Philosophy of Evil.*
PIOTR SZEWC, *Annihilation.*
GONÇALO M. TAVARES, *Jerusalem.*

Joseph Walser's Machine.
Learning to Pray in the Age of
Technique.
LUCIAN DAN TEODOROVICI,
Our Circus Presents . . .
NIKANOR TERATOLOGEN, *Assisted Living.*
STEFAN THEMERSON, *Hobson's Island.*
The Mystery of the Sardine.
Tom Harris.
TAEKO TOMIOKA, *Building Waves.*
JOHN TOOMEY, *Sleepwalker.*
JEAN-PHILIPPE TOUSSAINT, *The Bathroom.*
Camera.
Monsieur.
Reticence.
Running Away.
Self-Portrait Abroad.
Television.
The Truth about Marie.
DUMITRU TSEPENEAG, *Hotel Europa.*
The Necessary Marriage.
Pigeon Post.
Vain Art of the Fugue.
ESTHER TUSQUETS, *Stranded.*
DUBRAVKA UGRESIC, *Lend Me Your Character.*
Thank You for Not Reading.
TOR ULVEN, *Replacement.*
MATI UNT, *Brecht at Night.*
Diary of a Blood Donor.
Things in the Night.
ÁLVARO URIBE AND OLIVIA SEARS, EDS.,
Best of Contemporary Mexican Fiction.
ELOY URROZ, *Friction.*
The Obstacles.
LUISA VALENZUELA, *Dark Desires and*
the Others.
He Who Searches.
MARJA-LIISA VARTIO, *The Parson's Widow.*
PAUL VERHAEGHEN, *Omega Minor.*
AGLAJA VETERANYI, *Why the Child Is*
Cooking in the Polenta.
BORIS VIAN, *Heartsnatcher.*
LLORENÇ VILLALONGA, *The Dolls' Room.*
TOOMAS VINT, *An Unending Landscape.*
ORNELA VORPSI, *The Country Where No*
One Ever Dies.
AUSTRYN WAINHOUSE, *Hedyphagetica.*
PAUL WEST, *Words for a Deaf Daughter*
& Gala.
CURTIS WHITE, *America's Magic Mountain.*
The Idea of Home.
Memories of My Father Watching TV.
Monstrous Possibility: An Invitation
to Literary Politics.
Requiem.
DIANE WILLIAMS, *Excitability:*
Selected Stories.
Romancer Erector.
DOUGLAS WOOLF, *Wall to Wall.*
Ya! & John-Juan.
JAY WRIGHT, *Polynomials and Pollen.*
The Presentable Art of Reading
Absence.
PHILIP WYLIE, *Generation of Vipers.*
MARGUERITE YOUNG, *Angel in the Forest.*
Miss MacIntosh, My Darling.
REYOUNG, *Unbabbling.*
VLADO ŽABOT, *The Succubus.*
ZORAN ŽIVKOVIĆ, *Hidden Camera.*
LOUIS ZUKOFSKY, *Collected Fiction.*
VITOMIL ZUPAN, *Minuet for Guitar.*
SCOTT ZWIREN, *God Head.*

FOR A FULL LIST OF PUBLICATIONS, VISIT:
www.dalkeyarchive.com